CHANGE THE WAY YOU THINK ABOUT YOUR
FAITH AT WORK

A COLLABORATIVE RESOURCE BY IWORK4HIM

JIM & MARTHA BRANGENBERG
TED HAINS

HIGH BRIDGE BOOKS
HOUSTON

You have a calling. Have you heard this before? The job that you hold, the work that you do, the people that you work with, none of that is by chance. The people that you work with need to meet Jesus, and you may be their only chance.

—Jim Brangenberg, iWork4Him Show Opening

Don't copy the behavior and customs of this world, but let God transform you into a new person by changing the way you think. Then you will learn to know God's will for you, which is good and pleasing and perfect.

—Romans 12:2 NLT

Dedication

IWORK4HIM: CHANGE THE WAY You Think About Your Faith at Work is written and dedicated to the memory of the "old" version of thousands of working Christ-followers. I was once a working Christ-follower who had no idea what to do with my call to ministry. After spending years walking alongside guys like Os Hillman and our storyteller Ted Hains, I can say that God is living and breathing and active in my work. I am humbled that God had the patience to work it out in me. I hope that you will let God work out your workplace ministry calling in you too.

—Jim Brangenberg

Contents

Introduction

A SUCCESSFUL HIKE INTO the deep woods requires some useful tools. A seasoned hiker might suggest a compass, a GPS, or specific gear based on the terrain. Veterans even publish booklets to instruct and ensure a better journey. Any way you look at it, you need something to keep you on the right path and headed in the right direction.

Believers need tools and resources for our workplace mission field. We need a guide providing information and how-to's to live out our faith journey in our work. *iWork4Him* is dedicated to that effort.

iWork4Him is a statement of faith. It's a lifestyle that impacts everything we do. It is a permanent paradigm shift in our minds. Being able to say "iWork4Him" demonstrates a deepening of our faith. It is Jesus coming alive in us, in our work.

> Don't copy the behavior and customs of this world, but let God transform you into a new person by changing the way you think. Then you will learn to know God's will for you, which is good and pleasing and perfect. (Rom. 12:2 NLT)

So how do we live the iWork4Him lifestyle? How do we stop compartmentalizing our faith while doing our work? How do we apply Romans 12:2 and stop copying the world? We first go to the Bible as our primary resource because it is filled with God's wisdom and examples for living out our faith. We wrote *iWork4Him* as a secondary resource providing the practical, tactical, factual, and biblical resources on how you can live out your faith in your work.

For years, iWork4Him has had a front-row seat to the move of God in the workplaces of Christ-followers in America. We have heard the stories, conducted interviews, and covered the conferences and workshops that focus on this topic. We have gathered these stories and resources in this book to guide us on the path to saying iWork4Him.

You are called to work. It is a gift from God. He created work as a way for us to partner with Him. The workplace is the largest ministry opportunity in the world, and God wants you to join Him there. Let's get ready to go in the field—the mission field of your work. May this journey be life-changing. Permanently.

Ted Hains: Author and Storyteller

Each chapter of *iWork4Him* is enriched with a true story from the life of my (Martha's) dad, Ted Hains. Ted spent his career as a portrait photographer and recalled feeling much like Moses with a staff in hand, and asked God to use the camera he was carrying to fulfill God's plan for his life. He's passionate about using his gifts and talents for the Lord during retirement.

Ted is currently serving as a board member of iWork4Him Ministries, Inc. and Ambassador for iRetire4Him. He enthusiastically helps his peers learn to live the "iRetire4Him" lifestyle. Ted uses his newest hobby, woodturning, to open the door to conversations that lead to his faith. He is also a member of the Pocket Testament League, where he speaks on their behalf and passes out John's Gospel daily.

He and his wife of 64 years, Elaine, split their time between in Cass Lake, Minnesota, and Fort Myers, Florida. They have three daughters and one son, eight grandchildren and 14 great-grandchildren, scattered across the United States.

Always able to share an application, Ted has generously poured out his memories for our benefit. Ted lives with faith at the center. His professional career had many ups and downs by the world's standards, but he has chosen growth through adversity and success. Enjoy the look behind the curtain as Ted shares from his heart for our benefit. I am blessed to be his daughter and have had a front-row seat to this life well-lived.

Thanks, Dad, for being such a great example to me, our family, your employees, friends, and the people who will read this book. You and Mom have lived and worked through the filter of the gospel, and I am eternally grateful. I love you.

—Your Daughter,
Martha

I am grateful for your daughter and you, Ted. She is an amazing gift from God that you and Elaine stewarded so well.

　—Thank you,
　Jim

Before We Begin...

Before we begin, I must note that most of the narrative in this book comes from me, Jim Brangenberg. When I refer to "us," I'm referring to my wife, Martha, and me.

Part I

PART I OF *IWORK4HIM* brings you the practical, tactical, factual, and biblical ways to put your faith into action in your workplace, no matter how your workplace looks.

With each lesson shared and story told, we want you to recognize, celebrate, and declare "iWork4Him." This book is for you. You have influence, you have a ministry, and you can make a difference. While everything in this book applies to every Christ-follower living out their faith in their work, our focus is on the everyday believer, not the top influencer in their organization.

On the iWork4Him show, we have interviewed over 3,000 people living out their faith in their work. As we highlighted ministries and reviewed written resources for the show, we knew that God was calling us to feed the hunger for encouragement and challenge for the everyday believer, not the owners and leaders.

You will walk away challenged and equipped to impact your workplace mission field.

1

iWork4Him Spelled Out and Explained

IWORK4HIM—IT'S A statement about life, a declaration of faith, and a life plan. It is possible to work for Him, and it's a challenge worth choosing. To say "iWork4Him" confidently shows purpose in your work. Let's break it down.

i

Me, myself, and i. The i is lower case, making someone else the focus. This personal statement declares a conviction.

Work

God created work as a gift from Him. From the very beginning, He worked with Adam in the garden.

> So the LORD God formed from the ground all the wild animals and all the birds of the sky. He brought them to the man to see what he would call them, and the man chose a name for each one. He gave names to all the livestock, all the

birds of the sky, and all the wild animals. But
still, there was no helper just right for him.
(Gen. 2:19-20 NLT)

God gave us work to bring about flourishing to our
souls and not as a punishment for sin in the garden. God
created work first as a gift to you and me. Work is where
we meet people who are not like us and don't believe as we
do. It is the largest mission field on the planet. God created
work on purpose and for a purpose. You and I are designed
with a unique set of gifts, talents, and abilities to do our
work with excellence.

4

3 + 1 = 4 The number 4 represents Father, Son, Holy Spirit,
and You. Working for Him is a team effort. The three parts
of God teamed up with you. You are focused on Him in
your work, keeping your eyes on the Lord and His end
game. You don't work for your boss or yourself, not even
your family. You work 4 Him.

Him: Almighty God

Him with a capital H is our Heavenly Father. You and I are
image-bearers of the Almighty Creator, God of the Universe. He created you for work. God is a worker, and so are
you. Our focus is on Him.

iWork4Him

iWork4Him is a mindset and statement of faith. It's a revelation and a revolution. A revelation from God that our work matters to Him and He intended to work alongside us. It's a revolution against the status quo for Christianity. Most Christians are deactivating their faith when they get to work. Rules and fear squelch their witness for Jesus. However, God and a few of us Jesus-followers can radically impact our country through vibrant Christianity, the kind of radical Christianity that transformed the Roman Empire. Our Father has gifted us with the power of the Holy Spirit to bring radically good news to the lost we encounter in the marketplace. America's workplaces are the largest mission field we face. Many ministry opportunities exist in our workplaces because we work alongside so many who are lost and hopeless.

> *We ask God to give you complete knowledge of His will and to give you spiritual wisdom and understanding.*
> —Colossians 1:9 NLT

iWork4Him: When you surrendered your life to Jesus, you went through a radical transformation. You are a new creature in Christ. Everything about you is changing, including how you view your work and the people who work with you. Radical faith brought on by following Jesus is transformational.

Faith in Jesus transforms you and impacts everyone around you, even if they don't believe in Jesus. Transformational faith is changing the world one person at a time. Now it's time for your faith in Jesus to transform your workplace. Too many workplaces are devoid of Christians living out their faith. We can't give up our workplace territory to the enemy of our souls. It's time we stand up and shout for all to see and hear: "Here am I; send me! iWork4Him!"

Ted Hains Shares a Story: High School Hero

When I was a junior in high school, the Korean War was raging. Patriotism among my peers was running high.

Don Rough, a guy I played football with, said to me in the locker room one night after practice, "I am going to the Rock Island Arsenal to check out the Marine Reserves. Do you want to come along?"

I said, "Sure, when are you going?"

So the next Saturday, we jumped in my 36 Chevy Coupe and drove to the Arsenal. We were nervous as we walked through the doors of the Arsenal. I noticed the display cases of all the armament and war regalia and found it overwhelming. As I watched the Marines do their exercises and drills, I thought, *I'm not ready for this! I need to concentrate on my senior year.* I don't think I ever had that thought before.

By the fall, going into my senior year, our Marine Reserves had been called up to enter the fighting in North Korea. Before I graduated, I read in the *Rock Island Argus* newspaper that Don Rough had given his life in combat. I stood motionless on my parents' front porch for a long time after reading about Don's death. I had no tears and didn't know how to pray. The whole thing left me filled with emptiness. I found it very hard to go to school the next day. I knew I'd have to talk about it with all our football friends, and the teachers would ask about him. I didn't know anything. We'd never written. He and I were close, but we were guys. Don's death left me empty. Even now, at 88, I wonder what kind of man he would have been. I wonder if I would have told him about Jesus; I wonder if he would have had a family. Questions, lots of them. Yet I know, "And as it is appointed unto men once to die, but after this the judgment" (Heb. 9:27 KJV).

As often as I can, I hand out pocket testaments of the book of John. I realize I may only talk to someone once. We have no idea what tomorrow will bring. Today is the day of Salvation. *Today*! It keeps me running every day.

Bottom Line: We all have people we work around all day long. Will any of them die today? Tonight? Tomorrow? We can't let regret drive our lives. The enemy loves to use guilt to keep us from acting on our faith in Jesus. You can live your life with intentionality. Let those you work with know that following Jesus changed your life. Let them know God loves them and see what God does next.
www.iWork4Him.com/jointhenation

Chapter 1 Questions

1. Is today the first day you have ever heard that your work is a gift from God?

2. Did you know that your workplace is a mission field and a place of ministry?

3. How will this information change the way you prepare for work tomorrow?

4. Ted shares his emptiness following the loss of a high school hero because he didn't know if he was a Christ-follower. He uses this experience today to motivate himself to share the gospel when he is out in public. What motivates you to share the gospel?

2

Jim's Story – The Birth of iWork4Him

"BUSINESS IS BUSINESS, and church is church. They have nothing to do with each other. So make a lot of money in business and give it to the church, and maybe you'll serve on a committee one day." That one statement wasted 20 years of my potential workplace ministry. Let me share some of the stories leading up to this statement and the birth of iWork4Him.

1979 was a challenging year for our nation economically, but it was a pivotal year in my life. As a 13-year-old, I got up the courage to ask my parents for $300 and permission to go to a summer youth conference with our church. The trip came at a time in my life when I needed to make some life changes, and my parents agreed to write a check and let me go.

At the end of the conference, the speaker offered several challenges to the crowd. I knew I needed to go all-in with my faith, so I decided to commit to full-time ministry. I was ready to raise my hand in commitment when the speaker said, "Anyone who wants to commit their lives to full-time Christian ministry, please stand up and shout at the top of your lungs, "Here I am, Lord. Send me." As I hesitated to respond, I could hear the friends around me whispering, "Is Jim even a Christian?"

That night I stood up and committed my life to full-time Christian ministry. As a high school student, I gave my life work to God and assumed that I would someday be a youth pastor. Little did I know what God was going to teach me and how He would use my work. After the conference, my youth pastor and a young college student mentored me. They walked through life with me and helped me apply the Bible to my daily life.

A few years later, Martha and her family moved to Minnesota. We became fast friends and spent a lot of time together at church and leading Bible studies. After our first date, I knew we would marry. We discovered that we had attended that same youth conference in 1979 and made the same commitment to full-time Christian ministry. We assumed we would finish our four-year degrees and eventually go to seminary. Martha and I got married in 1986, I completed my Computer Science degree, and a few semesters later, she earned a Management Major and Accounting Minor. We were ready to put our degrees into practice. We are entrepreneurs at heart and loved sales, business, fixing problems, and answering customers' needs.

Martha's family was entrepreneurial, and I had been a practicing salesman since childhood. When I was eight, I started selling greeting cards door to door. I created a business reselling golf balls from the pond, selling hubcaps from the side of the road, and Ginsu knives at the state fair. My computer degree came from the practical side of the current economy, but we soon discovered that programming was too dull for me. I loved managing the people and the projects, and soon we started our own small business on the side.

I enrolled in seminary to stick to our commitment to God. Our senior pastor came to me and said, "Jim, there aren't enough laypeople out there within the church. We need more people who can volunteer. I also don't think you're cut out for full-time church ministry. You could never handle having 400 bosses. So why don't you stay in your insurance career and keep volunteering as a lay minister within the youth ministry." Lay minister became like a swearword to me as I felt less valuable than a paid pastor.

I was devastated. For the previous 10 years, Martha and I had thought that church ministry was in our future. I unenrolled from seminary, and we continued to volunteer. I didn't doubt that this message came from God, but it was hard news to take. During that time in my life, I had two business mentors. I talked to them about the decision not to go to seminary. They were phenomenal people, who were also great businesspeople, but they didn't understand a connection between faith and work. When I was about 23 years old, one of them said, "Business is business and church is church. They have nothing to do with each other. So make a lot of money in business and give it to the church, and maybe you'll serve on a committee one day."

That's how I was disabled as a Christian business guy. That message cut my feet out from under me. Multiple "Christian" businesspeople had mentored me to believe I should work all day long and make money to support the church and volunteer my time for ministry at night and on weekends. We loved doing youth ministry through the years, but the critical misinformation led me to believe, "Jim, your work doesn't matter. Just use it to make money."

I had all these skills and education but didn't see how God could use them.

Through our 20s, we sold insurance and used cars together. We were successful businesspeople who loved our work and our employees. But we kept thinking we were doing these tasks to support our church. We ministered to many of our clients, but we lacked the mindset to connect our faith and work.

To grow our business, we purchased a chain of insurance agencies; at the same time, we committed to become debt-free. Through the biblical principles taught by Crown Financial Ministries, we determined we did not want debt to stand in the way of anything God would call us to do. So that year was full of changes, including moving to a smaller town, a smaller mortgage, and starting our hike up the debt-free mountain. That same year, the doctor told Martha, "Your sinuses are a mess, and your circulation is bad. Most of your symptoms would improve if you moved somewhere warm near the saltwater. I would suggest Florida." Those were prophetic words.

We had only owned our 100-year-old insurance agency for six months when the doctor shared his powerful suggestion to move. We spent the next four years preparing to sell the agency. We learned more about living a debt-free life during that time, as God prepared our hearts to move to Florida.

I joked with my friends that at 37, I was planning my midlife crisis on my schedule. Little did I know that I must've made God laugh very hard with that statement. On my schedule and my terms. Right. ☺

We moved to Florida and immediately joined a church and small group where we became fast friends with Bob and Deanna Keator. I was still trying to determine my next career move when Bob gave me the book *Halftime* by Bob Buford. The book taught me that I could pursue significance in my success. I prayed, "Father, I've seen success. I would love to see success again, but I don't want to waste any more time. I want to pursue significance, and no matter what I do here in Florida, please show me the way to significance in my success."

Being a teacher and a car dealer was at the top of my newly created career bucket list. I was fulfilling a dream by continuing to run our used car dealership. We soon learned that our business model did not match the Florida used car model, and we knew a change was in the air. I took a job teaching math at a Christian school and spent the fall closing out the car dealership. Five weeks into the teaching job, I realized this would not be the last career move for me. But God used the teaching job to move me away from the car business to leave me open to the next opportunity. Each job was a turning point in my work and directed me closer to the start of iWork4Him.

My brother-in-law offered me a job that was a perfect fit and twice the pay. The only catch was he wanted me to start working for him right away. I told him I believed I needed to keep my teaching commitment until the end of the school year. So until then, I was a teacher by day and risk manager by night.

iWork4Him Begins

My job as the IT operations and insurance risk manager of a construction project started full time in mid-May 2006. My daily commute to Orlando took 90 minutes in the morning and 120 minutes at night. I committed the morning drive to learn how to pray. I started praying for my family, then my four bosses, their spouses, and their families. Later I added my co-workers and employees. I spent my morning commute praying through past hurts and bitterness and learning to intercede on behalf of those I love and serve.

My new job in Orlando used every skill I had developed in previous jobs. It was the best work of my life up to that time. Then my friend Bob, the same one who gave me the book *Halftime*, sent me a copy of the devotional *Today God is First* (www.TodayGodisFirst.com) by Os Hillman. These devotionals taught me that my workplace was my place of ministry. I had never heard this before. I began sharing those devotionals with others in my office.

> My workplace was my place of ministry.

At 40 years old, I had read through the Bible every year since my commitment at age 13, and *I had never heard from any pulpit or Bible study that my work mattered to God.* I learned I didn't need to work within the church's four walls to be in ministry. I began to realize that I was already in full-time Christian ministry. I was in ministry in a job trailer on a construction site in Orlando. The transformation didn't happen overnight, but my understanding grew as I read these devotionals and other books about the connection between faith and work. My eyes were opening, and God was using me as a minister in my work.

It was 2008, and I had a dream job in the construction industry. It was a challenging year, and by the next spring, we shut down the job site. We closed the company by the end of 2009. The best job I ever had just disappeared.

During these challenging months, I had the opportunity to pray with my bosses and staff many times. I took on the role of pastor in our workplace. It was such a great honor and privilege.

In late January 2009, one of my bosses and I flew to Iowa to deliver some layoff notices. After landing, we had a 90-mile drive in a snowstorm. We came over a hill at 55 miles an hour, and traffic was stopped. I slammed on my brakes, but the car wouldn't stop. I swerved to the shoulder to avoid hitting a semi-truck. We slid past the stopped traffic and down the shoulder another 150 yards.

We finally came to rest and saw a semi-truck full of pick-up trucks heading straight for us down the shoulder. If we had stopped on the freeway, we would likely have been crushed between two semis. The semi-truck driver took the ditch to avoid killing us and drove through the ditch and ended up on the shoulder directly in front of us.

My boss and I had argued about Jesus the entire plane trip to Iowa, so I looked at her and said, "We just about died. Somehow despite my most heroic efforts, I could not stop this vehicle. It's like somebody pushed us 300 yards so that we wouldn't die. It's not because of me, because I'm ready to go. But you're not. You need Jesus. Don't miss this opportunity. God preserved your life." My boss came to Christ later that year. That opportunity would never have come had I not already accepted my role as a minister to the lost in my workplace, including my four bosses.

God had been teaching me about the Holy Spirit. I read *Forgotten God* by Francis Chan and was struck by his statement, and I paraphrase, "If you are successful using your natural gifts, talents, and abilities, then you get the credit. But if God uses you to do something unexplainable from your natural gifts, talents, and abilities, then God gets the credit." After reading this, I told the Lord I wanted a job like that. I asked Him to use me in a way where He gets the credit.

Jobs were hard to find, and I started consulting and mentoring a local insurance agency owner. I launched a division of an IT company at the height of the recession. But God used my sales skills and my desire for relationships to make it a success. I needed to develop a massive network of relationships and joined a local BNI group. Dozens of meetings followed where I met with BNI members, prayed with them, and trusted that the sales would come if I put others first. God took care of the details as long as I met with people, shared my story, and prayed with them.

God was growing something new within me. I began studying how to disciple Christian businesspeople to understand their work's significance and uncovered God's maturing move in the marketplace, the Faith and Work Movement. I found many companies led by Christ-followers, Faith and Work ministries, and books on the subject. Along the way, I considered joining other organizations, but God kept telling me to wait. I had an executive summary written and told the Lord that I would know He wanted me to move forward with this ministry when He gave me a name for it. I had written a list of 132 company names, tag lines, and mission statements, but none of them registered with my soul.

One evening I knew it was time to move forward when God gave me the name iWork4Him. I knew it was from God; it was direct, straightforward, and creative. Under the name iWork4Him, I could disciple four or five Christian businesspeople at a time but asked God how I could challenge thousands of people. I had no platform to share. I wanted more impact than four or five people at a time. I purchased several iWork4Him websites and excitedly told Martha about it when she came home. But I still didn't know what iWork4Him was. I just knew we were getting close to what God wanted for our lives. It had been almost 10 years of God working on my heart and refining my job life.

In Tampa Bay, I had been part of a networking group that would later become the Christian Chamber of Commerce Tampa Bay. At our fifth anniversary gathering, I spoke on "Five ways to incorporate your faith in your workplace" and saw that it resonated with the audience. I sat down in the room next to Deborah Roseman, the only person I didn't know, and she said that I needed to share that message on the radio. I thought she was crazy. She repeated her statement, and I agreed to email her my executive summary for iWork4Him. Within the hour, she called me and reiterated the need to talk about iWork4Him on her radio station.

Martha and I met with Deborah to review the details and the costs involved to begin the one-hour radio show on Monday nights. I couldn't imagine spending money to talk on the radio, but as we walked out of the meeting, I told Martha, "This is the stupidest idea I've ever heard, but radio seems like the answer to our prayers. We prayed for a life of significance, a success that could only be attributed to God, and an opportunity to reach thousands with the iWork4Him message. I believe this is the answer to those prayers." So we said yes to radio and aired the first iWork4Him radio show on April 15, 2013.

In the first few weeks on the air, I imagined being the next great Christian Rush Limbaugh, espousing my great wisdom on all the listeners. My friend and C12 group leader Ross Harrop helped me to see that monologuing wasn't working. He suggested I use my skills to interview people, hear stories of Jesus-followers in the marketplace, authors focusing on faith and work, and people involved in the ministry of discipling others to live out their faith at work. Ross was right and sent by God. In week three, I began an interview format we still use today. I soon received compliments that helped me know that God was continuing to answer my prayers because it reached more people than imagined, and I had never had any radio training.

From the beginning, God gave me two significant directives to keep in mind as iWork4Him moved forward.

1. Don't reproduce the wheel.

2. Think big, very big, bigger than you can even think, or ask, or imagine.

The first directive kept me from starting a ministry that probably already existed. Our job was to make existing Faith and Work focused ministries famous and promote them to replicate. iWork4Him is to be a mouthpiece for the Faith and Work Movement.

The second directive from God is a constant challenge. I have never been described as a big thinker. I still don't know what God's bigger plan is, but He's done big things along the way, and I keep stretching myself to think bigger than I could ever ask or imagine (Eph. 3:20).

We slowly added more days to the show. When Tuesdays became available, Martha agreed to join me for

"Together on Tuesdays with Jim and Martha Brangen-berg." We discussed how the marriage relationship affects the workplace. People started to comment, "Jim, when you're on the radio, it's good. But when Martha's on the radio with you, it's great radio." We realized God called us to do this together. Our entrepreneurial days taught us that our skills complement each other, and we knew this was a journey we were taking together. I serve as the lead inter-viewer on the show, but Martha adds details and pulls the conversation together.

For the first few years, we worked full-time jobs and hosted the iWork4Him Radio show five days a week. At one point, we formed a business partnership to support the expansion of iWork4Him. We spent quite a bit of time talk-ing, praying, and fasting before we decided to move ahead with this partnership, but in the end, God said, "Enough! I want you to go all-in, stop trying to help me. I will provide for you. Trust me." We ended the business partnership and went all in.

God was using the broadcast and podcast to challenge people to live out their faith at work. We began traveling to conferences focused on the Faith and Work Movement. We interviewed Christian workplace believers from around the country, in big and small towns, capturing how they lived out their faith in their work. Our travels also helped us make connections across the Kingdom of God. God opened the doors to broadcast in additional cities too. In many cir-cles, we are called the mouthpiece for the Faith and Work Movement, where we focus on building collaboration and unity in the body of Christ. God has given us a bird's eye view of what He is doing in the workplaces of Christ-fol-lowers all over the United States of America.

At the time of this writing, we are digital-first with our long format show and producing a one-minute show played on stations across America. We took a summer sabbatical to finish three books: *iWork4Him*, *iRetire4Him*, and *sheWorks4Him*. We are working on a digital-first marketing platform to advance iWork4Him nationally to challenge all 55 million Christ-followers in their work. To help them recognize that their workplace is their place of ministry, their assigned mission field.

God has been working on this story my whole life. He has used even hard mistakes to make me useable today and shown me that I am not less than. My work is valuable, and He wants to use me in my work to be a minister. You, too, have a story to tell about how God has been preparing and using your heart for workplace ministry. We would love to hear it. www.iWork4Him.com/contact

Ted Hains Shares a Story: Korean War

I had just turned 10 when the Japanese thrust the United States of America into World War II by bombing Pearl Harbor. In a short time, five of my uncles and one cousin were in various military branches. Two of them ended up being pilots, one US Air Force and one in the US Navy. Flying became very important to me, and right after high school, I went to work for Ozark Airlines. They had nine DC-3s in their fleet. I was a station agent, and my job was to sell tickets, park the airplanes, get coffee, load baggage, and find out the weather. I often joked that my job also included "sobering up the pilots."

This job put me on the airfield in Moline, Illinois, and I couldn't have been any happier. Hearing and seeing airplanes taking off and landing all day was a constant thrill for me. I soon bought 1/10th of a plane and started taking lessons to become a pilot. That ended abruptly when one of the other 10 owners crashed the aircraft on a downstate Illinois field. A few days later, an executive from Ozark came to our little station and fired everybody. Getting fired caught me off guard. I asked for an explanation, and he said he caught the station manager running hot tickets. I wasn't sure what the executive meant until he explained that the station manager was selling tickets for non-scheduled airlines while Ozark employed him. That was a no-no, and the home office wasn't sure how serious the problem was, so we all had to go. End of story. At least that one. So I lost my job because someone else was cheating.

Bottom Line: I had a job I loved. I was grateful for it, and it brought me great joy. Someone else's behavior destroyed my career. I had a decision to make—grow bitter and angry or forgive and move on. Now that I am 88 years old, I am glad I chose the latter. No one knows what would have happened if I hadn't lost my job, but the incident didn't damage my heart with bitterness. How about you? Have you been unfairly hurt by someone else's actions in your work? Maybe even unfairly accused? You have two choices. "Love your enemy and pray for those who persecute you" OR grow bitter and angry. Please choose to forgive and love because it will set you free.

Chapter 2 Questions

1. My journey led me through many ups and downs and lots of adversity. Not every day was easy. What trouble is God using in your path to shape you into who He can use more effectively?

2. My commute changed my life through the power of prayer. How do you use your commute to grow in your relationship with our Heavenly Father?

3. Ted talks about losing a job because of someone else's dishonesty. Has this ever happened to you? While that isn't fair, how did it shape your character to make sure it won't happen again?

3

Martha's Story – In His Time

JIM HAS SUCH A fantastic ability to recall dates, the sequence of events, and all the factual details surrounding milestones in our God story. I'm so grateful for this gift, and it has lent itself to the celebration of some unusual anniversaries—first date, first kiss, commitment to ministry, etc. Jim also often refers to me as the co-host that gives color to the conversation. I can see how topics fit together, how people feel or need to respond, and our struggle to handle impromptu situations with grace. So this is my opportunity to fill in the color of Jim's telling of the accounts in our life.

Our lives are an open book, individually and together. God has continually shown us how to care for others' needs, teach others what we learn, and share our experiences openly.

On our wedding day, we themed our program "In His Time." Ecclesiastes 3:11 says, "He has made everything beautiful in its time. He has also set eternity in the human heart; yet no one can fathom what God has done from beginning to end" (NIV). God has shown that theme in our lives repeatedly. Has He done that for you?

- Jim and I are both the babies of the family whose parents started their faith journeys around the same time in life, in different parts of the country – *in His time.*

- We attended the same youth conference to hear a message that would solidify our lives of service, even though we had not yet met— *in His time.*

- On our first Sunday living in Minnesota, God directed my parents to visit Jim's family church—*in His time.*

- We became fast friends, finished high school, attended college, and were married at the ripe old ages of 19 and 20—*in His time.*

- Career changes, moves, babies, houses, churches, all part of the puzzle that God was piecing together—*in His time.*

Born into an entrepreneurial family, I have been involved in small business my entire life. My parents lived resourcefully, with attention to others as a theme in our home. Godly hospitality was a large part of my home life and served as a tangible example of God's love to others. From inviting stray teenagers to live with us for a season to sharing our faith and home for the employee Christmas party, there was always more room at the table for food, fellowship, and faith.

As a professional photographer, my father attended Christian Business Men's Connection (CBMC). He also learned from such men as Stanley Tam and R.G.

LeTourneau about committing his business to God and connecting his faith to everyday work. As a child, I translated this into serving the customer well, doing business with integrity, and giving God the glory.

My parents always centered our home activities around the church calendar. They supported many missionaries, housed them during their time home from the mission field, and took us to annual mission conferences. So when I made the commitment to full-time Christian ministry at a youth conference in 1979, it seemed likely that missions would be a part of my future.

Just a short time later, my parents felt God call them to make a change and to use the camera in my father's hand as a tool for the Kingdom in a new way. For them, that meant a one-year term in Venezuela, photographing the missions work there and then transplanting the family to Minnesota from Illinois to work at the Evangelical Free Church's headquarters. My parents shared their calling with my sister Mary and me (the youngest siblings at ages 16 and 14). They told us how they felt God was calling them but believed it was essential for us to agree and want to spend a year in a South American boarding school. We prayed and decided that this was what God wanted for us, and even began singing the song "I am Willing Lord" as a testimony to our path.

The time on the foreign mission field as a 15-year-old was very impactful and life-changing. I have an incredible appreciation for foreign missions and saw firsthand what families experience when they make such a big decision and uproot their families. I treasure this experience and only regret that I didn't better understand my everyday mission field—*in His time.*

The move to Minnesota continued the adventure that eventually led me to meet the love of my life—Jim Brangenberg. As friends in high school, we conducted Bible studies for church and school and worked at church camp together while sharing the love of Jesus. Once we were married, our Kingdom work continued. As entrepreneurs, we served our customers well, did business with integrity, took care of our neighbors, and volunteered at church in our free time. I can look at our past with great satisfaction, yet there is always the reality that something significant was missing. We didn't see our day-to-day tasks as Kingdom work, and we did not fully see our surroundings as our mission field. We still considered full-time ministry as a paid position, either in a church or on the foreign mission field. *In His time*, we would come to understand the more significant connection our faith could have in our life.

Jim has shared the chronological details of our life, so I'm just going to fill in a few more blanks. When we first moved to Florida, I took a job at an insurance company to provide a stable income as we settled. The work environment was oppressive, but I was determined to be salt and light for Jesus in an otherwise dark workplace environment. It had been a while since I had worked for someone other than our own company, but I knew that God wanted me to risk a few comforts, serve my employer well, and stand for my faith. After about one year, I took a job at our kids' Christian school, allowing me to be near them and much closer to home. Eventually, I transitioned to manager of the Christian bookstore for 10 years. Most people dream of working for a Christian organization, believing that they can *finally* do ministry. Many ministry opportunities happened in the school and the bookstore, but it shouldn't only be there.

I have found that many organizations are outward focused and forget about serving their employees and meeting their spiritual needs. Being primarily outward focused can lead to a toxic work culture inside of a ministry. So whether you work for yourself, someone else, a church, or other organization, take some time to look at what God has entrusted you to manage. Your mission field is right in front of you—your employees, vendors, customers, or clients. Treat them as your mission field and then they will know how to do the same within their sphere of influence.

When God stirred up the idea for iWork4Him and gave birth to the radio show, I was still working full-time at the bookstore. In my free time, I helped with social media and other details to help make it a success. Eventually, I became a regular part of the show, working together with Jim to share the truths we were learning regarding our workplace mission field. As God continued to grow the show, my career path took a few turns, first to run another business together and then full-time with iWork4Him. Those turns along the way were full of exciting change and painful lessons. God doesn't waste opportunities, and I believe He continues to show us that we have much to learn, *in His time*.

It had been more than a decade since Jim and I had worked together daily. God created us to complement each other with our skills. I love working with Jim and spending my days with him, but we needed to learn to dance together again. Through the ups and downs of starting a radio program, applying to become a non-profit, fundraising, securing outside vendors when needed, and producing a daily show, God has been teaching us the same lessons we talk about on the program. Our workplace is our mission field, and in that mission field, we may be the only Jesus our co-workers and employees ever meet. *In His time*, more Christ-followers will learn this truth.

From our very first date in 1984, Jim and I have ended every day together in prayer. Prayer is an integral part of our marriage, friendship, family, work, ministry, and life. Ultimately, this puts God in the center of our decisions as we seek His blueprints for our lives. Even though we are praying together, we still make plenty of mistakes. However, we learned to apologize, seek forgiveness, and then go back to God and ask Him for help. We carry this practice into our work environment as well. Each day, we start with prayer, seeking guidance for every decision we will make and the people we will encounter. Throughout the day, Jim and I often stop in the middle of disagreements to pray and ask God to help us sort it out. *In His time*, others will learn the power of prayer in their life and their work.

Every show, I ask myself this question, "What does this mean for the listener/reader?" When you listen to the iWork4Him podcast/broadcast, you listen and learn from our guests. You get connected to others who are also trying to connect their faith and work. And you are made aware of ministry organizations that are discipling Christ-followers to live out their faith at work. We want to share our experiences and connect and collaborate for the Kingdom, to equip more Christ-followers to live out their faith at work. We love to cover the stories of what God is doing in the workplaces of America. As we hear these stories, our faith is growing too—*in His time*.

It would be wonderful if the whole world loved Jesus, but how will they ever learn about Him if we don't live out our faith all day long in our work? Jesus saved me for more than Sunday. As we say on almost every show, "We all have a calling. Have you heard this before? Your workplace is your mission field, wherever that may be. You're either all in or all out—are you for Him? I am! iWork4Him! I work for Jesus Christ."

Ted Hains Shares a Story: Korean War —Adversity Never Wasted

The Korean War was on, and I needed a job. I truly wanted to fly. I went to the US Air Force recruiter, and before I knew it, I was on a train headed for San Antonio, Texas, and Lackland Air Force Base. It wasn't long until they were finding out who wanted to fly, and I certainly did. I took all the required testing: nearsighted, farsighted, color blind, and written. To say I was sad when I got my score was an understatement. I missed it by so little. Later, I found out that my mother was greatly relieved that I couldn't be a pilot like her brother. He had survived the Big War, but I think she prayed him through it. I always call my mother a world-class worrier.

A week later, I was called back into the CEO's office and told they had reevaluated my test and I could head for flight school right after basic.

Because of what my mother said about being relieved, I said, "Sir, I must respectfully decline."

He said, "Hains, you are crazy. This is an opportunity of a lifetime! Dismissed."

"Now what?" I said under my breath. Many of the guys had already been assigned to their training schools. There were very few things to choose from, so I decided to go to the air police school. I finished my basic training and was ready for my next assignment. Before I left Lackland Air Force Base, I had to go to the base chapel, the dentist, and several other offices. I gathered all my military records and the approval for my next assignment.

The final phase of the record collection process was in a large room with tables all around, manned by uniformed soldiers. The soldiers were there to check to see that all our records were in order so I could leave. I went to the very last table, and the sergeant sitting there looked up at me as he opened my folder.

He said, "Do you want to be an air policeman, son?"

I shrugged and said, "I got to do something."

The next thing I knew, he reached into my folder, took out my dental records, and threw them into the wastebasket. He said, "Your dental records are not in here. You're going to have to go back to the dental lab and get them."

One of the things I learned in the US Air Force was that you don't ask questions of those in authority over you. But I did wonder, *What was that all about?* After a long wait, I finally got my records from the dental clerk and returned to the debarkation center to find just a handful of guys. They told me to come back tomorrow.

Tomorrow came, and I went back to the debarkation center. I was packed, ready to go, and at the airfield at 1800 hours. Our destination was unknown. We flew all night, and as the sunrise was coming up, I could see mountains from the windows of the C46 aircraft. I was sure I was looking at Mount Rainier, so we would probably land at McCord Air Force base near Tacoma, Washington. We did.

As they escorted us to our barracks, they pointed out the location of all the important buildings, such as the mess hall and shower. As commanded, I reported to the C.O.'s office at 1000 hours the following day. I went in, not knowing what to expect. I snapped to attention and gave my best military salute.

He said, "Stand easy, Hains, have a seat if you like."

"Wow," I thought, "What a difference. I think this will be OK."

"I've been looking at your file. I see you worked for Ozark Airlines."

"Yes, Sir," I said.

"What did you do for them?" I told him, and he said, "That sounds a lot like base operations to me. Would you like to do that here?"

I said, "I don't know what that is, Sir."

"It's in that small building down there on the flight line. Tell them I sent you. You're to hang around a couple of days and see what they do. If you like it, come back and report to me, and I will get you started. Oh, and don't forget to read the manuals while down there."

It didn't take long for me to realize I could do this job, and it was second nature to me. I just had to add a few things to what I already knew and forget about "selling tickets." I became an aircraft dispatcher for the next three and a half years.

Through all this, I learned two life lessons. First, I believe there are angels assigned to guide and protect us. Second, Jeremiah 29:11 is true: "'For I know the plans I have for you,' declares the Lord, 'plans to prosper you and not to harm you, plans to give you hope and a future'" (NIV). The sergeant who threw away my dental records ultimately had a hand in my safety. The delay prevented me from being assigned as an air policeman, which could have cost me my life.

Also, the bad stuff I had heard about the military wasn't always true.

Bottom Line: So often, when we are in the thick of things and we don't see the end game, we doubt God is in control and making our paths straight. I am sure about one thing regarding my assignment for the Korean War. My life was likely spared by not becoming a pilot. I gained valuable skills at the airport job that I loved and lost; God had a plan to use those skills. He used the adversity in my life to prepare me for the US Air Force. God has a plan for you when you let Him lead; you will not be disappointed.

Ted Hains Shares a Story: Engaged and Headed Off to War

I was engaged to Joyce, a beautiful student nurse. However, the War was going on in Korea, and I was about to leave for an island in the Pacific. I traveled to San Francisco to pick up my orders. It was a beautiful sunny day when I climbed the ramp to the deck of the troopship USS General Mann. Over the P.A. system, a very tiny tone came through with Jo Stafford singing, "Though I fly the ocean in a silver plane, I belong to you." This song, "I Belong to You," put a little bounce in my step as I remembered my girl back home. There was so much uncertainty flowing through my mind as we cruised under the Golden Gate Bridge, and for the first time, I realized the enormity of the ship I was on and the trip ahead of me across the Pacific Ocean.

A few days out, we ran into bad weather that continued to worsen. As the soldiers and airmen were getting sick, the Marines had to lock down the heads so nobody could use them. *"If you're gonna throw up, ya better head to the railing!"* That's how it was. All of us were on the railing, heaving our guts out and laying on the deck, moaning. As I remember it, more than one marine got puked on that day, but they still had to stand their post.

The mess hall was open, with the tables raised to standing height. If you could eat, the food would slide all over the hard metal surface of a table.

At night we had to stay in our rack (sleeping quarters). We were piled five men high. I slept on the top bunk. Often in the middle of the night, I could hear the garbage cans sliding across the steel flooring, which was all that separated me from the Mess Hall overhead. After another day or two, the weather got worse, and we headed into a typhoon. It split a large gap in the side of our ship. There was never a concern of the ship sinking, but it was mighty uncomfortable. During that time, I ran into a marine from Rock Island who was my closest friend's brother. We only had a brief conversation, but I sensed his fear as he realized he would be on the frontlines of a battlefield in a few days.

Our ship slipped into Yokohama for repairs, which allowed us to see the surrounding country. There I met my first Japanese people. A few years earlier, our country taught us to hate the Japanese. They were the enemy because they had bombed Pearl Harbor only 10 years ago. I had to put my prejudice aside and ended up having a great day ashore with the people of Yokohama.

Bottom Line: Often, as we prepare for a job and get mobilized for our next assignment, some storms and delays try to disintegrate our determination. For me, it was a trip across the Pacific. What is it for you? In the form of adversity, the storms are there for us to learn about the power of God. When you are in a storm, try to see God's hand of purpose in it.

Chapter 3 Questions

1. Martha talks about our journey, "In His Time." What is the most important thing to recognize about His time vs. our time?

2. Jim and Martha learned the hard way that being in full-time ministry didn't always mean being in a pulpit. Most people in ministry are nowhere near a pulpit. What does your workplace ministry look like?

3. Ted talks about his assignment in the US Air Force. He thought he would go in one direction, but God directed his steps and put him in a place that utilized the skills gained in the job from which he got fired.

   a. Has God made your path straight as He directed you to a career in the past?

b. Did you recognize His hand in the process?

c. How do you see His hand now in your work?

d. Please describe a time when your job put stress on a meaningful relationship.

e. What kind of prejudice influenced you as you grew up?

f. How has that prejudice impacted you in adulthood?

4

The Lies We've Swallowed About Work

THE ENEMY OF OUR soul uses lies to keep us quiet and ineffective in living out our faith in our work. For me (Jim), these lies shaped the better part of 40 years of my life. Since you are reading this book, I suspect some of these lies may have shaped your life too.

Lie #1: Work is work, and church is church. They have nothing to do with each other.

In my early 20s, two of my mentors spoke this lie into my life. They didn't mean to teach me this lie. It was modeled to them, and they modeled it to me. That's how the enemy works. He is a deceiver. Work and church, or work and Jesus, have everything to do with each other. Your work is given to you by God. He designed you with a unique set of gifts, talents, and abilities to use in your work for His glory.

The lie assumes that our faith keeps us from success and making money. The lie asserts that if we live out our faith in Jesus, we will accomplish less because living a life of no compromise would mean settling for less. If you have lived believing this lie, it impacted the way you treated people. Don't get caught up in regret. Ask the Lord to forgive you for operating under this lie, and additionally, ask forgiveness from those you took advantage of or mistreated. You can't go back and relive those years with this new knowledge, but you can move forward in your work and have it impact everything from now on.

The truth: Work and Church (Jesus) have everything to do with each other.

Lie #2: Keep your faith at home because of the separation of church and state.

In 1802, Thomas Jefferson wrote a letter about a wall of separation between the church and the state. The intent was to protect the church from the state, not protect the state from the church. You see, Thomas Jefferson understood the government is a threat to the church, and protections need to be in place. However, this protection is misapplied in today's anti-Jesus world. The lies read: *"Leave your religion at home. It has no place in the workplace or government!"* Our founding fathers formed this country on biblical principles to allow the free expression of religious faith as a core principle for our country. They knew that Jesus and the Bible gave life to all the activities of a nation, and a nation without Jesus and the truths of the Bible would be a nation bereft of morality. You have the right to live out your faith in your work. There is no place that you can't take your faith. The United States, without the Church (Jesus), is a mess.

The truth: Your faith belongs with you everywhere you go.

Lie #3: You are a second-tier citizen in the Kingdom of God if you aren't a pastor or missionary.

This lie might look like: "If you truly want to make an impact in the Kingdom, then you need to be a pastor or a missionary." Until I was 40, I believed this lie. "If you already have a job and you feel called to the ministry, then quit your job, go to seminary, and serve in a church somewhere."

The Kingdom of God maintains no ranking system. Even if you are not a pastor of a church or missionary overseas, you can still impact the Kingdom of God. Your ministry is at your place of work. You are not a second-tier citizen in the Kingdom because you aren't a pastor or missionary. I believe most of you are pastors or missionaries in your work and no one ever told you.

Each one of us has a calling. Some get called to be a pastor or a missionary. However, most of us get placed in a job that fits our calling out in the marketplace. So if you have been looking for a place on the mission field, What about your workplace? Isn't it filled with people who need Jesus?

The truth: God called and ordained you as His missionary to everyone you meet, even the person in the cubicle next to you.

Lie #4: The American Dream is biblical truth for Christians.

The American Dream is *not* biblical, and it is not guaranteed. It emphasizes material ownership, vacations, and living a life of leisure. The charade of the American Dream distracts us from God's best for us in life. When Christians live a life focused on pursuing the American Dream, many miss God's best for their lives and get burdened by their possessions. You may have noticed that your local four-walls church has struggled with this as well by dreaming of larger congregations and bigger buildings instead of solving community problems.

We are so focused on giving 10% and keeping 90% that we forget that it is all God's. I remind myself often that everything I accumulate, such as houses, cars, clothing, and toys, will end up in the landfill one day. Will this perspective help you?

What would the world be like if all the Christians in America pursued Jesus instead of the American Dream? For instance, how does the pursuit of this dream impact our ministry in our neighborhoods? For us, it meant neglecting the building of neighborhood relationships because we were so busy working to keep up with the Joneses. The pursuit of the Joneses kept us from experiencing deeper relationships.

It is nice to have possessions, and there is nothing wrong with them. But the more you have, the more they own you, taking your time and attention. Suppose you used debt to purchase your stuff; paying the loan fuels the nightmare further. Our stuff keeps us from loving on the people we care about most. Will it be more possessions or deeper relationships that bring you more joy at the end of your life? When you invest your relationship time in those around you, then you will experience the real dream.

The American Dream of retirement happens to be a lie too. You can learn more about that in *iRetire4Him: Unlock God's Purpose for Your Retirement*. This lie says, "At the end of my career, I can sit back, relax, and stop working. I will have peace and life will be *good*." Jesus taught about this lie in the following parable.

> A rich man had a fertile farm that produced fine crops. He said to himself, "What should I do? I don't have room for all my crops." Then he said, "I know! I'll tear down my barns and build bigger ones. Then I'll have room enough to store all my wheat and other goods. And I'll sit back and say to myself, 'My friend, you have enough stored away for years to come. Now take it easy! Eat, drink, and be merry!' But God said to him, "You fool! You will die this very night. Then who will get everything you worked for?" Yes, a person is a fool to store up earthly wealth but not have a rich relationship with God.
> (Luke 12:16-21 NLT)

Jesus' parables always teach lessons. In this parable, what point is Jesus trying to teach us? He's saying that self-focused living can cause us to keep things we may never be able to use. When we focus on gathering possessions, we miss the deep relationship God has for us.

The truth: Building a relationship with God and others leads to a fulfilled life.

How Do These Four Lies Impact Our Work?

Living under these four lies strangles our faith and renders it virtually irrelevant. The world doesn't have time for another religion of money, power, and control. The lies above describe just that sort of religion. However, that religion looks nothing like what Jesus asked of His followers.

Following Jesus is about a Divine rescue plan for rebellious children. It is about bringing honesty, truth, hope, and love to a lost world. It is about selfless living. Following Jesus is about being transformed to be like Him. It's not about rules and regulations. It is about grace and mercy. It's not about meeting in a building on Sundays; it's about *setting the church loose on Sunday to bring about healing on Monday through Saturday.* Following Jesus isn't about you; it's all about Him. It's about realizing that no matter what I think I know about life, He knows better.

When these four lies infiltrate our work and businesses, we allow the enemy to decide where ministry takes place in our lives. For 20 years as an entrepreneur, I did not see myself working in my ministry sweet spot. I saw myself as a man working hard to donate money and time to support those called into *real* ministry. I was there to finance them. Wrong! While they were doing great work, worthy of our financial support, the pastors and missionaries we supported never met the people I met. The people I met daily were put into my life on purpose because I had a relationship with them, and I had something they needed, hope in Jesus—The Way, the Truth, and the Life. It was my opportunity through relationships to introduce them to Jesus. I missed many opportunities.

The Holy Spirit empowers us to be like Jesus. He is our life companion to help us put our mouths where our faith is. He is our guide, our counselor, and our access to the supernatural power of God. If our faith lacks power, we haven't accessed the spiritual power plant living inside of us. The Holy Spirit is the unfair advantage given to us by God.

He will help us live out a lifestyle where we can say iWork4Him.

The four lies highlighted in this chapter are just that— big fat stinking lies that almost destroyed my spiritual walk in the marketplace. But I don't live under these lies anymore, and you don't have to either. In the Name of Jesus, right now, I pray that the Lord will release you from the power of these lies in your life so you will be free from them forever. *Amen.*

Ted Hains Shares a Story: Korean War— Robert E. Lee

We left Yokohama, Japan, as soon as our ship was repaired, and headed on to Okinawa. Upon arrival, somebody showed me my quarters, a leftover World War II Quonset hut, complete with cockroaches and bugs of all types and sizes. They issued us DDT bombs to combat the bugs. Who knew how that would affect us!

I met Corporal Robert E. Lee, who was the company photographer in my squadron. He was a nice guy who didn't smoke, drink, or chew like most other guys. There was something special about this guy. On weekends, most of the guys would head to the village to get drunk (We didn't know about drugs; they were to come with the next war ... Vietnam) or shack up. Bob didn't do that. He said to me one weekend, "There's a Youth for Christ rally on the base. Would you like to go with me?"

"Sure," I said. It brought back memories of gospel meetings and Bible drills.

I had been in Okinawa for over a year when "the letter" came from Joyce. Yes, the one that starts with *Dear John*. It deeply wounded me. Devastation wracked my heart, and I got angry. I felt the pain deep in my gut and had to do something about it. I grabbed her photograph and a clip of 30mm ammo with my carbine rifle. I put her photo on a hillside and filled her face full of holes.

My friend Robert E. Lee got a Dear John from his wife. He didn't shoot her picture. His reaction drew me even closer to Jesus Christ. Robert helped put my life on a new course. Now over 60 years later, I realize what a man of God can do even when pressed down from every side. Robert was an excellent example for me. (*Oh, by the way, I carried the guilt of how stupid I had been to shoot my ex-girlfriend's picture full of holes that night. When I told a psychiatrist about my concern, he said, "In your given circumstances, you did the healthiest thing you could have done."*)

However, Robert taught me, "*You can live above your circumstances if Jesus is Lord of your life.*" For decades, I have searched military records to try to find Robert E. Lee so I could thank him. I had no idea how many Robert E. Lee's there are. God put Robert in my life for just that time. I can't wait for that reunion one day in heaven.

Bottom Line: I didn't know it at the time, but God used my time in the military to change my life direction. From planes to photography and from Joyce to Elaine. Now married almost 65 years, I know God allowed that time away in Japan to shape me into the man who would one day put all my trust in Jesus. What about you? Are there people in your life that God has used to impact you and shape you into the person you are today? Have you thanked them?

Ted Hains Shares a Story: Korean War— A Career Decision

It was one of those beautiful days when the sky is as blue as the ocean is vibrant, and I was standing in a chow line at the air force base in Okinawa, Japan. The line started at the top of the hill and ran down to the Mess Hall. From where I stood, I could see the Pacific Ocean. I stood in this line too many times to count, but it became a great place of contemplation for me.

I remember one time while waiting in line, reading the *Stars and Stripes Army Newspaper*. There was an article about two medics in North Korea. One medic was a conscientious objector, and the other one was his twin brother, who was told by their mother to "stay together" even though the US Army discourages that. The paper describes how one twin, Edwin, had gone out to pick up wounded soldiers. During the next shift, his brother Irwin came upon a mortally wounded soldier that died in his arms. It was Edwin, his twin brother. They were my friends and had lived just across the alley from me in Rock Island, Illinois. (That was six decades ago, and I can still hardly talk about it even as I write this.) As I stood in line, the story caused me to pause and made my heart hurt. At that time, I had already lost three friends in the Korean War.

As I returned to reality in the chow line, I realized I was alive—surrounded by beauty and by the sound of the chatter of airmen standing in line. I asked myself, "What am I going to do about all this? God has me here for a reason. Nobody's getting killed here." That was my prayer. I had always prayed as part of my Lutheran upbringing. You can do a lot of thinking in a chow line. I guess you can find yourself praying too.

Occasionally we were given passes to leave the air base in Okinawa. I loved to visit a little village south of Naha Air Base called Itoman. I liked to go there because it was a very primitive place. Men wore straps of cloth across their waist and sandals on their feet. Women wore what I would call a brown sheet for a dress. I often saw them with a stalk of bananas or bags of rice on their head. As I trekked through their village, they seemed not to notice me.

I would walk the streets, photographing things that my eyes had never seen before. One time, I was at the water's edge, and a group of men was pushing their fishing boat to the shore with primitive nets and fish lying in the bow of their hand-crafted vessel. At the end of a long day of self-guided tours, l had Kodachrome slides ready to send off to the lab in Hawaii.

One day as I boarded the local bus with livestock inside and rode the dusty trail back to Naha Air Base, I realized it had been an exhilarating day. I had photos in both black and white film in my Rolleiflex camera and Kodachrome in my Contax 35mm camera. I enjoyed my day as if no time had passed at all. I made it back to base just in time to get in the evening chow line. That gave me time to think again.

Up to that point in my life, I thought I would be a Lutheran pastor, but now this exciting new photography experience was beckoning me in a different direction. I rationalized that I wasn't a good enough student to make it all the way through seminary, so I decided to be a photographer.

After I finished my tour in Okinawa, I returned to the states and spent about another year at Scott Air Force Base near St. Louis, Missouri. I spent my free time researching photography schools and decided on the Ray Vogue School of Photography in downtown Chicago.

I realized that I was at a crossroads in my thinking: ministry or photography? Making that decision was easy for me: I prayed about it (the best I knew how), and I felt total peace about making the decision. Taking photos filled my soul with passion. I loved it. I think God helped me make that decision at a time in my life when I needed direction. I know today I can bring everything to God because I know that He cares about me. Ministry doesn't just happen in the pulpit! It occurs wherever He places you. For me, it was in photography!

Bottom line: I learned to take advantage of my thinking time. My quiet time with God was often in lines while I was in Japan. God spoke to me and filled my heart with His desire to serve Him in a lifetime of photography ministry. I am so blessed to have figured that out at an early age. God has a plan for you. Can you see all the steps He has guided you in so far? Quiet time isn't defined or structured for me. It is a time where I seek Him and listen. I do it every day. What about you? Do you have a quiet place where you can seek Him every day?

Chapter 4 Questions

1. Which lie has impacted your life the most?

2. What happens when we let these lies infiltrate our lives as Jesus-followers?

3. Ted shares that God used an inner passion for photography to guide his steps toward a career that would shape his entire life. What passions do you have rolling around in you that could end up being a career?

5

The "Theology" of Work in Non-Seminary Language

DO YOU DREAD MONDAY? Have you been tempted to call in sick on Monday because you couldn't face going to work? I recall a Garfield TV show where Garfield talked about the world without Monday. At first, he celebrated its elimination and then discovered Tuesday took its place, etc. In his comic strip, Garfield constantly bemoans Monday. What about you? Is Monday cursed or a day to be celebrated?

The home impacts our view of Monday. My father complained about Monday. He hated the traffic. He didn't like his bosses. My brother and sister always stressed out of their minds doing homework for Monday. (I probably should have been more stressed, oh well.) I got raised in a Monday moaning family. This chapter contains many references to ideas that flow directly from www.Work-Life.org.

As an adult, I love working. I love being busy, dealing with the challenges of the day, and interacting with people. Yet the Monday struggle is real. For me, my Monday struggle starts on Sunday night. After dinner, I struggle with a depression sinking over me, knowing that my life is not my own, and on Monday, the rat race starts all over again. I often moan and complain to Martha and beg the Lord to lengthen the weekend. However, I learned from Garfield you can extend the weekend, but Monday is always coming. So what do we do with all this?

- How do you act on Sunday night?
- Do you find yourself complaining?
- Do you find yourself cramming in last-minute projects you have been putting off?
- How does the Lord view your attitude about Monday?

Two thousand years ago, Saturday was the Sabbath and the work week started on Sunday. The first day of the week was different, but do you think they treated it any differently? I bet not. We have grown up in a culture that has celebrated Friday and bemoaned Monday. This mistaken celebration is where our theology needs a little work.

What did God do on the first day of the week? He created. God celebrated and created and called it good. Why do we call it bad if He calls it good? God created both Monday and Friday. Technically, Monday was the second day of the week, and God called it good too. God's crowning achievement, and His most incredible source of joy and consternation, was created on Friday, the sixth day when God created man and woman. He called them very good.

Here is a Bible nugget for you. On the very first day Adam was alive, was it a workday? Nope, Adam's first full day on the planet was a day of rest. God didn't create Adam and put him immediately to work on a "Monday." God first taught Adam to rest. Adam rested his first full day, and he did it with God in the garden. So often, we miss the significance of this. We are so busy thinking about our to-do lists or work that we miss two critical points in the creation story.

1. God is a worker.

God created for six days straight. Look at the vastness of what He made. He created galaxies that stretch 4 billion light-years in all directions. That's 186,000 miles a second times 31 million seconds in one-year. Over 5.8 trillion miles in one year times 4 billion years. Now that is pretty big! The galaxy is so vast that the light we see in the nighttime sky can be from stars that no longer exist.

He created the complex heavens and earth in one day. Consider the complexity of our self-replenishing earth with naturally reproductive traits, including a self-cleaning feature. The human body is even more impressive than the galaxies. In designing and creating everything, God shows He is a worker. He loves work, and He loves creating. He loves when you work, create, flourish, and subdue the earth. God created us in His image, which explains why we love to work.

2. God gave work to Adam.

God told Adam in Genesis 1, "Be fruitful and increase in number; fill the earth and subdue it. Rule over the fish in the sea and the birds in the sky and over every living creature that moves on the ground."[29] Then God said, "I give you every seed-bearing plant on the face of the whole earth and every tree that has fruit with seed in it. They will be yours for food.[30] And to all the beasts of the earth and all the birds in the sky and all the creatures that move along the ground—everything that has the breath of life in it—I give every green plant for food." Work was created by God, demonstrated by God, and then passed on to humanity. Then God said, rest first.

Understanding these two points is critical to living a Jesus-following life, especially following Jesus in our work. You might have grown up believing that work resulted from sin entering our world. If you and I think sin caused work, we end up thinking that the only kind of work God loves is ministry work from the pulpit or the mission field. This wrong theology is a twist of the enemy to neuter the followers of Jesus, the children of the Almighty.

God created and assigned work as a gift to Adam and Eve to tend the most fantastic garden in the world. God did more than keep them busy. He gave them purpose and caused them to flourish.

Adam's first work assignment was to name all the animals. God came alongside Adam in this work by bringing the animals to him, and then Adam gave them names. God assigned Adam work, and then He joined Adam in that same work to make it successful.

Don't miss these steps:

- God gave Adam a calling and work to fulfill the calling.

- God gave Adam a task to complete.

- God joined Adam in the task.

- Together they were successful.

God is a worker. He loves work and made us in His image to love work too. God joins us in the work we do. If He did it for Adam, He will do it for you. There are other examples of this same process throughout Scripture: Abraham traveling to Canaan, Joseph ruling Egypt, Paul spreading the gospel to the Gentiles, etc.

Wouldn't these topics make a great sermon series? Or better yet, a sermon centered around the whole matter of equipping the saints (Eph. 4:12)? Imagine a church that sees itself as a manufacturing plant producing Monday morning workplace believers in their mission field? Until I was 50 years old, I never heard sermons on business, the marketplace, or how God feels about my work. I now know that God is a worker. He blessed work and makes it possible for us to flourish in our work. God has an assignment for you, a calling. He wants to work beside you every day. Do you let Him?

I love this verse:

> For we are God's handiwork, created in Christ Jesus to do good works, which God prepared in advance for us to do. (Eph. 2:10 NIV)

He created us to do good works prepared for us long ago. How can we do good works while moaning and complaining along the way? God created us to do good works with a unique set of gifts, talents, and abilities. That means we are designed uniquely for our work.

So what is the purpose of church on Sunday? It is our retooling day at the manufacturing plant. We get fed spiritually and connect with other believers for refinement. Sunday is the launchpad for our Monday morning mission.

The sermon prepares us to go into our mission field of service to God in our work. Attending church is for all ministers of the gospel to get equipped and sent out in their called mission field. Every Sunday is a sending service.

If we spend our lives focused on the weekend, we may miss the people God connects us with during the week. If we focus on the celebration of relaxation and ignore the fulfillment of work, then we worship what the world glorifies and overlook the purpose God gave all humanity.

> *Thank GOD! He deserves your thanks.*
> —*Psalm 136:1 MSG*

Romans 12:2 says, "Don't copy the behavior and customs of this world, but let God transform you into a *new* person by changing the way you think…" (NLT, emphasis added)

TGIM (Thank God it's Monday) vs. TGIF (Thank God it's Friday) is a significant shift in our thinking to celebrate work instead of celebrating relaxation. We can bring change to our work through the attitude we carry today. Make the Monday switch (www.Worklife.org). Commit to living a No Moan Monday lifestyle and start celebrating going to church on Sunday as the launchpad to your mission field. The Holy Spirit's power can help us make these adjustments. My friend Dr. Jim Harris taught me that the Holy Spirit is our Unfair Advantage in the workplace to help us.[1]

God created work as a gift for us, and work is an act of worship. The Hebrew word *Avodah* means "work, worship, and service." So what was God's plan behind our work? His plan was for our work to be worship—or you might say "workship." Our work becomes worship when we do it for God's glory. That is the foundation for the word *work* throughout the Old Testament.

The ancient Hebrews had a deep understanding of how faith and work intersected in their lives and used the same word for work and worship:

> *Our work becomes worship when we do it for God's glory.*

- "Six days you shall work (*Avodah*)…" (Exod. 34:21 ESV)

- "Man goes out to his work (*Avodah*) and to his labor until the evening." (Ps 104:23 ESV)

- "This is what the LORD says: Let my people go, so that they may worship (*Avodah*) me." (Exod. 8:1 NIV)

- "But as for me and my household, we will serve (*Avodah*) the Lord." (Josh. 24:15 NIV)

Work is a gift from God, and it's also worship. Here's what we know from Scripture about work:

- God created us to do good works – Eph. 2:10.

- God wants us to enjoy our work – Ecc. 3:12-13.

- God created all the days – Gen. 1:31.

- God created work before the fall – Gen. 2:15.

- We need to stop copying the behavior and customs of this world and let God transform us by changing the way we think, especially about work – Rom. 12:2.

- Our work is worship – "workship" Col. 3:23.

Ted Hains Shares a Story: You're the First to Know!

It was 1954, and I was about 22 years old. I got discharged when the Korean War was over. I went to the Vogue School of Photography and applied for the GI bill. Then I got a pretty good job as a parking attendant for the Allerton Hotel (a historical city landmark located on Chicago's Magnificent Mile).

To start, I worked the third shift at the Allerton Hotel, from 11 p.m. to 7 a.m. The first few hours were hectic, but then it went still about 2 a.m. after the Shay Peri (a famous Northshore dance hall) down the street closed for the night. I was in a small shack on the west end of the parking lot, as the other entrance was closed for the night. This parking lot was the only one in the entire system that was open all night. All the parking lot employees brought in their money at the end of their shift and put the money in the floor safe slot.

I got paid every other week. I had been working for about 10 days when things started getting rough financially. My GI bill hadn't come through yet, the school wanted more money, and my rent was coming due. I was flat broke with no other options, and I wasn't going to ask my parents for any more help.

As usual, it was getting lonely at about 3:30 a.m., and I was bored. I looked around for food because sometimes the other attendants left a sack with cookies or bananas or something that I could eat. I saw a bag placed on the window ledge. It was bulky, so something was in it ... cash! Lots of *cash*! I was so startled. I pulled it away from my face. There was so much cash, more than I had ever seen in one place. I almost threw it to the desk; ideas raced around in my head faster than I could imagine. Pay my rent, pay my school bill, and eat a decent meal—too many thoughts! I don't know if I screamed it out loud or only in my mind, but I had to say "Stop ..." I can't do this. It's not mine!

I quickly stuffed it down into the safe where it was irretrievable. I was so relieved that it was over. No one will ever know the thoughts I had in my mind that evening, but I can tell you my integrity was in danger.

"No one will ever know." Those very words I'd said in my head just moments earlier reminded me of the story of Joseph in the Bible when he ran from his master's wife as she grabbed his cloak. Many decades have passed since that night. I've often wondered how taking that money could have changed my life. It was a crossroads moment for me. I wonder what I would have given up if I had kept that bag of green paper.

> For the love of money is the root of all kinds of evil. And some people, craving money, have wandered from the true faith and pierced themselves with many sorrows. (1 Tim. 6:10 NLT)

Bottom Line: C. S. Lewis once said integrity is doing the right thing even when no one is watching. I believe God was watching me that night in the parking lot. My life could have gone in one of two directions. My integrity held me on the straight and narrow. In your work today, is your integrity driven by your faith? As a Jesus-follower, our uncompromising integrity is just one reason people ask, "What is different about you?" New clothes might not fit right all the time, but integrity fits just right every time.

Chapter 5 Questions

1. When I learned that God wanted to work alongside me, it changed my life. He never intended for us to slug through our work life without help. What did you learn that shifted the way you think about work?

2. Are you a TGIF'er or a TGIM'er? I spent the first 20 years of my career celebrating Friday. How about you? Can you celebrate both?

3. Ted found a pile of cash and no one around to know if he took it. He recognized it as a crossroads in his life. He chose well. When have you been presented with a huge ethical dilemma? How did you react?

1 Harris, Dr. Jim. *Our Unfair Advantage: Unleashing the Power of the Holy Spirit in Your Business.*

6

The 7 Costs of Working 4 Him

Don't copy the behavior and customs of this world,
but let God transform you into a new person by
changing the way you think.

—Rom. 12:2 NLT

THINGS OF VALUE HAVE a cost. A business decides to purchase a building instead of leasing space based on a cost analysis. We give up revenue to hire qualified employees that help our organization grow. These benefits come at a cost. When we give up something for Jesus, the cost of following Him has long-term benefits. My iWork4Him journey revealed seven impactful costs. You may experience different costs in committing your work to the Lord. I know there will be costs, but every cost you face will be worth it.

Scripture sets the stage to learn about worthy costs. In Romans 12:2 above, Paul says we need to let God transform us into a new person, by changing the way we think. As we read, pray, grow, and learn, it's essential to allow God to be the transformer. He will help us to think like Him and not like the world. In Matthew 5-7, Jesus laid out the costs of following him in our work when He preached the Sermon on the Mount. Take a few minutes right now to grab your Bible and read those chapters before you go any further here. Note the costs and the benefits that Jesus mentions.

Cost #1: Give Up—Wrong Thoughts

Sinful thoughts run freely in our minds and afflict many of us. Jesus addressed this issue head-on in Matthew 23:27 when he called out the Pharisees and labeled them white-washed tombs. They looked good on the outside, but they were dead inside. Our sinful thoughts can leave us dead inside too. The good news is that Jesus is there to help us with these thoughts through the Holy Spirit. As you learn to follow Jesus in a way that influences those at work, it's no longer an option to look good outside but be a mess inside.

> *But I warn you—unless your righteousness is better than the righteousness of* the teachers of religious law and the Pharisees, you will never enter the Kingdom of Heaven! (Matt 5:20 NLT, emphasis added)

Our wrong thoughts cause us to drift away from where God wants us to be. Giving up wrong thoughts may seem simple, but it can be the most difficult to do. My wrong thoughts are often judgmental. I pray about it, and I think I am doing better until I get behind the wheel of a car, and the judging comes out again.

Just the other day, I was on the main road here in Ft. Myers, Florida, and a driver in front of me made a left turn from the right-hand turn lane. I find myself talking to these people out loud in my car. I criticize their driving and call them names. It's possible they were lost and realized it at the last minute, but a safe U-turn would have been a better option. Talking about others behind my car's wheel is just one way I find myself having negative thoughts. I also talk to the newscasters on TV. They churn up all kinds of viciousness inside of me. That's my story; what is yours? Where do you find yourself being critical and having ugly thoughts about people?

When I judge people, I often miss who the real person is on the inside. Once we get to know an individual, an image-bearer of God, we see His amazing hand in their lives. Getting to know people may not be possible when you drive down the road, but it is possible with those in your workplace.

Judging others may not be your thought-based struggle, but whatever your mind battle is, God wants to bring you internal healing. A clean mind is a place God can use more effectively in our workplace mission field. iWork4Him is a lifestyle and a statement of faith, and giving up wrong thoughts is one way to put that faith into action.

Let's reread Romans 12:2 and see the miracle God provides for our minds.

> Don't copy the behavior and customs of this world, but let God transform you into a new person by *changing the way you think*. Then you will

learn to know God's will for you, which is good and pleasing and perfect. (emphasis added)

Our thinking can change, and this verse tells us that God can do that. We can hear the very voice of God. Let go of the old way of thinking and watch your faith grow.

Cost #2: Give Up—a Double Life

As Jesus-followers, consistency in our behavior should be a hallmark of our lives. We should be the same person wherever we go, honoring Jesus all the time. I used to live one way on Sunday and Wednesday night and another way for the rest of the week.

As a young manager, one of my direct reports was a single mom who often had kid distractions at work. She was a believer and knew I was too, but there was conflict. She said I was condescending and arrogant, and unfortunately, I was. One day her car broke down and I used my expertise to get her a great deal on another vehicle.

After I helped her, she remarked, "Jim, why are you being so nice to me?" She was referring to my double life. At work, I was a jerk. Outside of work, I let my faith loose and served others. I have never been the same since she spoke those words into my life. I tried to find her recently to ask forgiveness for the pain I caused her but haven't been successful yet.

Are you struggling with living a double life? Some of the most valuable human qualities include authenticity, transparency, and vulnerability. Jesus consistently demonstrated these qualities, and we can too.

Pre-believers can tell a phony from a mile away, and living a double life is fake. Authentic living allows others to see the work God is doing in our lives. They will know why they should surrender their lives to Jesus as well. Imagine if we put aside our pride and openly showed our struggles. The Apostle Paul did this well, and he wrote about it in many of his books in the New Testament.

Here's Jesus' perspective:

> You are the light of the world—like a city on a hilltop that cannot be hidden. No one lights a lamp and then puts it under a basket. Instead, a lamp is placed on a stand, where it gives light to everyone in the house. In the same way, let your good deeds shine out for all to see, so that everyone will praise your heavenly Father.
> (Matt. 5:14-16 NLT)

Cost #3: Give Up—Unforgiveness

Unforgiveness defined the first 40 years of my life as I struggled with bitterness and anger. It is often said, and attributed to many different people, that "bitterness is like a poison pill we take, hoping our enemy will die." I took that pill for years. Bitterness is perhaps the most self-destructive human emotion. It can impact your health and keep others from wanting to be around you. The root is often unforgiveness, and unforgiveness had ruled my life.

Forgiveness is something most Christ-followers take for granted. We love the fact that we are all forgiven by Jesus. But when someone sins against us, we don't want to extend the same grace, even if they are family, friends, or neighbors.

See what Jesus says about it:

> But I say, love your enemies! Pray for those who persecute you! In that way, you will be acting as true children of your Father in heaven. For he gives his sunlight to both the evil and the good, and he sends rain on the just and the unjust alike. If you love only those who love you, what reward is there for that? Even corrupt tax collectors do that much. If you are kind only to your friends, how are you different from anyone else? Even pagans do that. But you are to be perfect, even as your Father in heaven is perfect. (Matt 5:44-48 NLT)

> If you forgive those who sin against you, your heavenly Father will forgive you. But if you refuse to forgive others, your Father will not forgive your sins. (Matt 6:14-15 NLT)

Why is giving up unforgiveness a cost to living out the iWork4Him lifestyle at work? Forgiveness is the hallmark of Jesus's rescue plan for humanity. When we demonstrate forgiveness to those who have hurt us, we show in a small way what God is offering every human on the planet.

Think of the impact on our workplace when we demonstrate forgiveness. Many of us know what it is like to work in a place governed by grudges and unforgiveness. We call that a toxic work environment. When we forgive those who hurt us and ask forgiveness of those we hurt, we replace toxicity with love.

I've been a manager in several organizations over the years. When you are a manager, you deal with people. When you deal with people, you are going to deal with hurt feelings and conflict. I can't count how many times I have had to ask for forgiveness from one of my employees. Usually, it was completely unintentional, but occasionally it was because I yelled or spoke out of turn. I have gotten pretty good at seeking forgiveness. I would much rather be humbled than to embitter someone. Whenever I get a new employee, I immediately let them know that I want them to tell me right away if I ever hurt them with my words or actions. I never intend to hurt them, but I want to deal with the pain I caused right away if I do.

Jesus came to set us all free from the bondage of sin. He wants us to let go of the bitterness and hurt so we can be set free and lead others to freedom. When we do, it attracts others to Jesus. Everyone around us wants to be free from bitterness and pain; your life will show them how to be free when you model forgiveness.

Forgiveness isn't easy, but it can be simple. If we believe and act on Jesus' words from Matt 5 and 6, it will change the way we think. He was serious about forgiveness, and now it's our turn.

Cost #4: Give Up—Damaged Relationships

My past is peppered with damaged relationships. For years, I counted on future opportunities to make new friends instead of dealing with the pain of resolving conflict. I moved on from broken relationships, pretending it didn't bother me, but they were hindering the growth of my faith and my reputation as a follower of Jesus.

The world is small, and I often encounter people from my past. I realized it was time to walk the path of reconciliation, deal with the hurt, and repair relationships.

I prayed and asked God to reveal the relationship carnage of my past; the list was long. I reached out to people and asked for forgiveness. Some responded positively, some reacted negatively, and some didn't respond. In 2005, I had destroyed a 20-year-old relationship. My friend had hurt me, and instead of talking it through, I stormed out and launched a verbal torpedo.

Later, the Lord reminded me of all the great things in my life because of this one friend. I was humbled and tried to call him, but his phone number changed. I sent a letter asking forgiveness and thanked him for all the great ways God had used him in my life. I never heard back, but I know that I said what needed to be said. My actions caused hurt. I could have set an example back in 2005 by seeking to have an adult conversation, but instead, I destroyed a relationship.

Pre-believers are watching Christ-followers and our relationships. If our relationships look broken and dysfunctional, just like the world's, what hope do we offer them? Jesus came to heal broken relationships, especially the one with our Heavenly Father. As you live out your faith at work, consider reconciling with those with whom you have damaged relationships. Seeking to repair old relationships may extend outside the workplace to family, kids, grandkids, former co-workers, old neighbors, people from church, and anyone else you've hurt.

Jesus expects peaceful resolution and reconciliation in the relationships of his followers. When we demonstrate reconciliation in our own lives, especially in those relationships at work, people will begin to experience Jesus through you. When you ask forgiveness of all the people you have hurt in the past, you will experience unprecedented freedom. Jesus talked about repairing relationships in Matthew 5.

> So if you are presenting a sacrifice at the altar in the Temple and you suddenly remember that someone has something against you, leave your sacrifice there at the altar. Go and be reconciled to that person. Then come and offer your sacrifice to God. (Matt. 5:23-24 NLT)

Ask God to reveal damaged relationships from your past. Someone probably came to mind as soon as you read this sentence. Typically, these are the people you argue with in your head. When God reveals a damaged relationship, quickly try to bring forgiveness into the relationship. You will find healing for yourself and others when damaged relationships are repaired.

Cost #5: Give Up—Hoarding Wealth

A hoarder is someone who keeps it all for himself. It's a worldly trait, not a biblical one. As followers of Jesus, we are to live a generous life as Jesus did. He demonstrated the ultimate generosity when He gave up His life for you and me. Hoarding keeps us from experiencing the joy of generosity, and it puts a roadblock in your testimony at work.

After Martha and I had been married for almost 13 years, we took a class on the biblical principles of money and possessions from Crown Financial Ministry. The course taught us, "You have been blessed 'financially' not to increase your status of living but to increase your status of giving." This statement is not bashing people who have nice stuff, but it's to keep money from becoming their master.

You may be asking yourself what this has to do with iWork4Him. Jesus modeled generosity. If we are stingy and slow to share, we look just like everyone else in the world. Generosity in the workplace might be fair wages, staying after work and helping a teammate, or taking up a collection when a co-worker has an unexpected expense.

Martha and I had to learn to live with an open hand. In our car business, we made it a practice to be generous with our repairs and maintenance. We found freedom in giving extra, even when it went unnoticed. When a customer asked why we went above and beyond, it allowed us to share our values. A life of generosity will enable you to experience independence from your possessions. Jesus came to set us free. Free from sin and free from allowing possessions to own us. Generosity is a way to be truly free. Jesus said it best in Matthew 6.

> Don't store up treasures here on earth, where moths eat them and rust destroys them, and where thieves break in and steal. Store your treasures in heaven, where moths and rust cannot destroy, and thieves do not break in and steal. Wherever your treasure is, there the desires of your heart will also be … No one can

serve two masters. For you will hate one and love the other; you will be devoted to one and despise the other. You cannot serve God and be enslaved to money. (Matt. 6:19-21, 24 NLT)

Give up hoarding and live a life of generosity, and you will attract people to Jesus.

Cost #6: Give Up—Worry

At 19 years old, I memorized the following passage from Matthew 6. Little did I know how much that would help me later in life.

Therefore I tell you, do not worry about your life, what you will eat or drink; or about your body, what you will wear. Is not life more than food and the body more than clothes? Look at the birds of the air; they do not sow or reap or store away in barns, and yet your heavenly Father feeds them. Are you not much more valuable than they? Can any one of you by worrying add a single hour to your life?

And why do you worry about clothes? See how the flowers of the field grow. They do not labor or spin. Yet I tell you that not even Solomon in all his splendor was dressed like one of these. If that is how God clothes the grass of the field, which is here today and tomorrow is thrown into the fire, will he not much more clothe you—you of little faith? So do not worry, saying, 'What shall we eat?' or 'What shall we drink?' or 'What shall we wear?' For the pagans run after all these things, and your heavenly Father knows that you need them. But seek first his Kingdom and his righteousness, and all these things will be given to you as well. Therefore do not worry about tomorrow, for tomorrow will worry about itself. Each day has enough trouble of its own. (Matt 6:25-34 NIV)

When I lost my job in the construction industry during the Great Recession, I lost past wages and it took me almost a year to find another job. I had a choice—I could worry or I could believe Jesus' words. I decided to believe Jesus. Over the year, without a steady job, I found part-time work and contract work. We never missed a meal or a house payment. When I balanced the checkbook, I would shake my head and say, "God, I don't know how you did it again this month, but I am grateful.

The many years of the Great Recession were challenging, but I look at them fondly because God provided miraculously for our family. Trusting God's provision over worry is not a guarantee for excellent health and great wealth but an exercise of faith.

Our lives as Jesus-followers are supposed to be defined by a new way of living and thinking. Worry is the old way, not the new way. Jesus said he would take care of us, and he will. The Bible is full of stories of provision, and I have been able to share my story of God's provision during unemployment many times. Do you have a story to tell?

When we find ourselves worrying, it sends the wrong message to those around us. When we worry, we communicate to others that we doubt the power of God. When we demonstrate our trust in the Almighty God of the universe, it encourages others. We give others a glimpse of His eternal love and provision by not worrying but wearing our belief in God for all to see.

We can deny God's power and allow anxiety to rule our lives or trust Him and live in peace. Demonstrating this trust in our lives, especially in our work, attracts people to Jesus.

Cost #7: Give Up—Hurry

Be diligent and productive, but never be in a hurry—don't miss those people the Lord puts in front of you. See the opportunities to serve while working, shopping, networking, building community, and while at lunch with a friend or co-worker. Hurting people are everywhere, and we can be there for them. Learning not to be in a hurry all the time has been a hard lesson for me. I am always busy and often in a hurry. I have learned that the incidents where people cause me to be late are often the people who most need me now when I am in a hurry.

A few winters ago, Martha and I were out on a date. It was late, and we were in a hurry to get home. On our way home, I noticed something weird on the sidewalk in front of our local citrus grove. I discounted it and drove on. About a mile later, I said to Martha, "We need to turn around. I think I saw someone on the ground back there."

We turned around, parked the car, and walked up the sidewalk to see what was happening. As we approached the scene, we discovered a woman had fallen from her bicycle and was bruised and hurting. She had wrecked her bike and was in no shape to ride home. We put the woman and her bike in our van and took her home.

We talked with her for a long time. She was hurting and was living in an unpleasant place. She had many addiction issues and uncovered a life damaged in a home where her father never showed her love. We stayed in touch with her for years but eventually lost touch. We got home really late that night but learned never to be in a hurry, because someone might need us.

Jesus was always busy but never in a hurry. People were his business. As you learn to live out the iWork4Him statement of faith and lifestyle, people are becoming your business too. In your workplace, you will have opportunities to be Jesus to people if you are available for them. Show up to work early, eat lunch with them, and don't blast out the door at the end of the day. When the pressure is off, people will share real life with you. Don't miss the chance to minister to someone by being available. It just takes a little intentionality.

Jesus' brother James wrote:

> What good is it, dear brothers, and sisters, if you say you have faith but don't show it by your actions? Can that kind of faith save anyone? Suppose you see a brother or sister who has no food or clothing, and you say, "Good-bye and have a good day; stay warm and eat well"—but then you don't give that person any food or clothing. What good does that do? So you see, faith by itself isn't enough. Unless it produces good deeds, it is dead and useless. (Jas. 2:14-17 NLT)

Is your hurried life keeping you from touching the lives of someone who needs to meet Jesus? Take a deep breath and notice the people you connect with all day long. Take time to know them and see what God does next.

There are costs to following Jesus and learning to live out the iWork4Him lifestyle. Every one of these costs sets us free. We can be free from the bondage of this world and open to doing the will of our Heavenly Father. You may have been a Jesus-follower for a long time, but you are still learning to follow Jesus. We all are. When we accept the costs of working for Him, our lives will be an attraction to pre-believers in our workplace, and our relationship with our Heavenly Father will strengthen. The benefit is priceless.

Ted Hains Shares a Story: Stanley Tam, R.G. LeTourneau, and Me—90%, 10% or 100%

Early in my career as a young portrait photographer, one of my heroes was Stanley Tam, founder of U.S. Plastics Corporation. I had seen him at a photographers' meeting when he told us how he had been in total despair, realizing he was a terrible salesperson. As I understand the story, he and God got very well acquainted one day when Stanley pulled off to the side of the road and screamed to God for help. He told God that he would give 90% of his earnings for ministry and keep 10% for himself. He started States

Smelting in Lima, Ohio, and he was extremely successful. I used his company for recycling the silver from the photo development process.

Another hero was R. G. LeTourneau. R. G. came to our little Evangelical Free Church in Moline, Illinois, to visit his daughter, who taught our Sunday school class. When her daddy preached that night, he got my attention by telling us that after several bankruptcies, he promised 90% of his earnings for God's work and he would live off the remaining 10%. As a young Christian, I heard, "You can make deals with God, and He will prosper you." Yikes!

By the 1970s, my portrait business was quite profitable, and color photography was just at the threshold of its beginnings. I owned a successful color lab that processed my film and made the prints for my photography business. The quality was excellent, and I naively thought I could expand it to serve the entire industry. I cleverly called it "Creators Custom Color Lab" with a lower-cost division called "Lab X." I was going to give 90% of the profits to 10 different Christian organizations and live on the other 10%. Wow. What a great idea! But we never made a profit. I was subsidizing the lab from the studio.

My routine was to get up early before the family and go to the studio and sit in my car in my parking space behind the studio, which I called my prayer closet. After praying for many things, I always ended with, *"God, I'm doing this for you, please make it successful."*

This routine continued for nearly seven years and disintegrated on April 1. It felt like any other day: prayer in the car, walk through the studio, out the front door, and to the side door, and up the steps to the laboratory. When I went up the steps, the usual bustling sounds or the noise of equipment running and people talking were absent.

That day, there was only quiet. It was so quiet I could hear the silence. I walked from printing room to printing room—nothing but silence. I looked in the job folders. Empty. No work to do. Every room was empty. From the back of the laboratory came the lab manager, saying, *"April fools! But this is no joke. I have returned every new order to the studio that sent them to us, I have gotten new jobs for all of your employees, and I have a new job myself, which I'm going to right now."*

Wow! I did not see that coming. I went back to my prayer closet and started praying again. It's as if I could hear a voice in my head. *"I never asked you to have this business, Ted. The thing I have been telling you is to be the leader of your home."*

I left a message for Joanie, my secretary, to cancel my appointments for the morning. I went home and told my wife Elaine what happened. Then I told her what I felt God was telling me. I said to her, "I am supposed to be the leader of the house." Elaine said, "I'm not sure I can trust you to do that. I'm doing a pretty good job, myself. I'll have to think about it."

I knew I would have to change. What does that mean? Would it mean that I would need to stick around and help at breakfast time? Would I have to deal with spilled milk, squabbling at the table, and all four kids talking at once? Would I have to help with the homework? Oh no, I'm not good at that.

After a couple of weeks, Elaine finally said, "Okay, I'll trust you." As a result of being obedient, all our children, three daughters and a son—and now all our 28 family members—are followers of Christ.

Bottom Line: When we try to help God, it often goes poorly. But when we submit to God in humility, it can end much better. Do you have a story of trying to help God? Maybe today, you can start over on a path of obedience to God. Are you willing to give God 10%, 90%, or all 100%?

Chapter 6 Questions

1. Which cost do you find hardest to surrender in following Jesus in your work?

2. Which one do you find the easiest to give up?

3. For me, it is helpful to have heroes of the Faith and Work Movement so I have examples to follow. Ted had Stanley Tam and R. G. Letourneau. Everyone's faith story is so different, but we need to find one that inspires us to keep going every day. I tend to look up to D. L. Moody because of his never-give-up attitude. Who do you look up to, besides Jesus, for modeling in your faith?

7

The Commitment and Covenant to iWork4Him

GOD USED MY 180-MILE roundtrip commute to reveal how I was to minister in my workplace. God gave me an outline of how to do that ministry. Amazingly, I have found at least three other organizations that use the same workplace ministry pattern. Like me, you may be wondering how to get started living out your faith in your work. I hope you are saying, "I want my life to scream 'iWork4Him,' and I want to make an impact on others through my actions and attitude at work." I am so proud of you. You now understand the significance of your ministry in the workplace.

Sure, it's nice to earn a paycheck, but in the grand scheme of things, the job you hold, the work that you do, and the people you work with, none of that is by chance. The people you work with need to meet Jesus, and you may be their only chance. Adopting the iWork4Him lifestyle is about transforming your workplace and the workplaces of the 55 million Christ-followers in the USA into a mission field. Recognizing this fact about your work is significant.

Like me, you may have considered quitting your job so you can go into full-time vocational ministry. Now you know you don't have to leave because you are already on the mission field. You already have a ministry, and it's full of people who need to know who you know, Jesus. Here are some easy steps God taught me to launch my ministry at work. I hope they help you too.

1. Prayer

Pray for my co-workers and/or employees by name each day.

As God helped me to better understand the connection between my faith and my work, He taught me about the power of prayer. First, I learned to pray for those I worked alongside every day. It made a difference. Did it change them? Not necessarily, but it changed me. It changed my heart. It helped me understand my role as a pastor and missionary to them.

When I started to pray for my co-workers, employees, and my bosses by name every day, along with their spouses and their children, I began to see them the way my Heavenly Father sees them. Praying for others changed my life by changing my heart. It was life-changing when I prayed for those I worked with that I didn't like.

After you have prayed for your co-workers/employees/bosses for a while, let them know. I usually mention that I have been praying over a casual conversation. Here is what I say, "I have been praying for all the people I work alongside, which includes you. Can I pray about something specific for you?" Usually, they will give you something to pray about very quickly. I start to pray as they asked me to pray, and that allows me to follow up on that prayer request one or two weeks later. When you stick with your commitment to pray for those you work around, God will begin to open doors of opportunity for you to minister in your work.

2. Care

Find a way to serve my co-workers and/or employees outside of what my job requires me to do.

When all you do at work is meet expectations, nobody notices. When you get your job done and find a way to lighten a co-worker's load, people start to notice. My specialty is organizing messy places. Almost every office I have worked in over the last 30-plus years has a cluttered closet or office that is considered the dumping ground of junk. This dumping ground collects garbage electronics and unused office furniture and desk accessories. It usually is storage for old brochures and out-of-date forms too.

Most of my jobs have been in management, and straightening the office falls under someone else's job descriptions. But I love to help clean up messes and bring order to the workspace. I have often grabbed a team and tackled the chaos, bringing peace to a formerly cluttered space. There were times of the year with lots of policy renewals in our insurance agency, and it was overwhelming. I recall surprising my team by staying late with them, working shoulder to shoulder, and ordering pizza. We all worked hard to catch everyone up. Examples like these catch people's attention and let them know that you care for them. Note that this kind of extra work often happens outside business hours because those hours are committed to your regular job.

How can you serve those you work alongside, over and above what's in your job description? Look around you. Do you see anyone nearby with an overwhelming amount of work? Identify someone overwhelmed with a project or task. Bring hope to them by helping them finish. When you stand out from the pack by serving others over and above expectations, others will notice and ask why.

Find a way to befriend my co-workers and/or employees outside of the workplace so they will trust me when I share the Truth.

Job relationships are often shallow. When you take that relationship outside of the office into your home, those relationships can grow. There is nothing like sharing a meal at your dinner table to get to know someone. When you get to know them better, you also get an opportunity to share who you are—including who Jesus is in you. Relationships give us a platform for sharing what Christ has done in our lives. We must earn that right.

For about two decades, Martha and I ran an insurance agency. We always put people through a rigorous hiring process with multiple interviews. Once we were sure we would make the job offer, we always invited the prospective hire and their spouse/significant other over for dinner. Casual conversation over the dinner table is the best way to know if you are making the right hiring decision. Over dinner, you can also share openly about who you are. Conversations about your faith are always acceptable as you share personal stories over food.

After hiring new team members, we continued having meals with them at least annually to stay in touch personally and let them know we cared. We always did this in our home because it was quieter with less stress and no time limitation. When our employees were over, they knew our focus was on them. We would host a family gathering in the summer and a couple's gathering at Christmas. These relaxed times together build deep relationships.

What will it be for you? How will you deepen your workplace relationships? Dinner in your home may work for you, but get creative and do something that suits your style. If you are stuck, I would love to brainstorm with you. Just email me at Jim@iWork4Him.com.

Remember, when you invite someone to your home, it says something special about you. You can set the rules, including praying over the meal. Your home is a temple of God. The Holy Spirit in you impacts those who enter. Your friendship will affect them and allow you to minister to them in a more profound way than a casual work friendship.

3. Share

Look for opportunities to pray with people at work when you notice they are having a tough day.

I have been practicing this since 2008, and I am always amazed at the power in that prayer. Just last week, Martha and I had dessert with one of my old bosses. When we said goodbye, she said, "I'm not leaving until you pray for me!" Of course, Martha and I prayed with her and her husband. Why did she insist on prayer? We have been praying together since long before I led her to Jesus in 2008. Prayer has become a part of our relationship.

This step involves putting your faith out in the open and on display. We often spend more time with people at work than we spend with our families. We get used to people and their usual daily demeanor. When you notice a change in their typical behavior, ask them how they are doing, then pause for their answer. If they say they are fine, use the movie line definition from the Italian Job, "Really? Freaked out, Insecure, Neurotic, and Emotional? How are you *really* doing?" and then listen for their real explanation. Once they share, then you can say, "Thank you for sharing that with me. Would you mind if I prayed about that with you right now?"

I've never had anyone refuse an offer of prayer. When someone is hurting enough to share something personal with you at work, they are open to prayer. When someone experiences adversity and pain, they start to think, "Where is the hope?" and "There must be more to life than just existing." Your co-workers/bosses/employees will welcome the prayer at a weak and vulnerable time in their life.

There is power in prayer. Real Power. After praying, I often look for a chance to share a copy of the Gospel of John with them. When someone reads the Word of God for themselves, they can know who the real Jesus is. That is why I am a leaguer. The Pocket Testament League (www.PTL.org) can help you get pocket testaments of the Gospel of John to share.

4. Work

Work with excellence—be the best and brightest example of a worker in your workplace position.

As a Jesus-follower, everything about us should be changing for the better. Everything. Especially in our work. When people know that we are Jesus-followers, they expect a difference in us. They don't know why, but they expect us to be "good." Excellence in you attracts others to our Heavenly Father. In your work, be a person of excellence in your attitude and actions.

Our attitude about others, our workload, our benefits, our bosses, and our environment speaks volumes. When we express gratitude in our words, it attracts others to the excellence in our attitudes.

We don't often see excellence in action at work. When you encounter a server, a salesperson, or a customer service agent with over-the-top treatment and care, that's excellence. As Jesus-followers, excellence should describe everything about the work we do. No matter what our workplace is, we should be the number one employee in our position. Complete your work and meet or exceed the established standards. Because we are Jesus-followers, we have everything to live for, and it shows in the excellence on display in our work. Let's strive to receive "exceeds expectations" on the next performance review and do excellent work today.

As a person of excellence, these words describe our character:

1. Loving
2. Caring
3. Courageous
4. Diligent
5. Fair

6. Full of Integrity
7. Respectful
8. Responsible
9. Trustworthy

Following these steps can allow us to share the hope we have in Jesus. As Jesus-followers in the workplace, when we display the attitudes and actions noted in these steps, others will be begging to know what is different about us. Our relationship with our Heavenly Father will naturally flow out of our lives and bless theirs. Whether they believe in Him or not, your life will draw them to the Truth.

The world sees work through sinful eyes. God keeps reminding me:

> Don't copy the behavior and customs of this world, but let God transform you into a new person by changing the way you think. Then you will learn to know God's will for you, which is good and pleasing and perfect. (Rom. 12:2 NLT)

Read the iWork4Him Nation Covenant on the next page and launch your workplace ministry today. God has been waiting for you. The iWork4Him Nation isn't a club you join, for you are already a family member of the body of Christ. You are finding out now that living the life of iWork4Him highlights some of the added benefits. God loves your work. He wants to work alongside you in it. Invite Him to join you.

The iWork4Him Nation Covenant

My workplace is my mission field, a place of full-time ministry. My workplace ministry manual is my Bible. My calling to my workplace is not a second-class calling. I dedicate my workplace as a mission field for God, and because of Jesus in my life, I am committed to celebrating the work that God gave me.

AS A MEMBER OF THE IWORK4HIM NATION, I COMMIT MYSELF TO:

- PRAYER

  - Pray for my co-workers and/or employees by name each day. (1 Timothy 2:1-5 (NLT) 1 I urge you, first of all, to pray for all people. Ask God to help them; intercede on their behalf, and give thanks for them.

- CARE

  - Find a way to serve my co-workers and/or employees outside of what my job requires me to do. (Galatians 5:13-14 (NLT) 13 For you have been called to live in freedom... use your freedom to serve one another in love. 14 For the whole law can be summed up in this one command: "Love your neighbor as yourself.")

  - Find a way to befriend my co-workers and/or employees outside of the workplace so they will trust me when I share the truth. (Ecclesiastes 4:9-10 (NLT) 9 Two people are better off than one, for they can help each other succeed. 10 If one person falls, the other can reach out and help. But someone who falls alone is in real trouble.)

- SHARE

  - o Look for opportunities to pray with people at work when you notice they are having a tough day. (Matthew 18:20 (NLT) 20 For where two or three gather together as my followers, I am there among them.")

  - o Be ready to share the hope that is in me, Jesus. (1 Peter 3:15 (NLT) 15 Instead, you must worship Christ as Lord of your life. And if someone asks about your hope as a believer, always be ready to explain it.)

- WORK

  - o Work with excellence – be the best and brightest example of a worker in my workplace position. (Colossians 3:23 (NLT) 23 Work willingly at whatever you do, as though you were working for the Lord rather than for people.)

Signature: _____ Date: __/__/__

www.iWork4Him.com

This covenant can be joined and downloaded online at www.iWork4Him.com/jointhenation.

Ted Hains Shares a Story: Almost Broke, but Bankruptcy Is Not an Option

It was the early 1970s when my lab manager decided it was time to call it quits on the color laboratory I dedicated to God. He was right, but I was conflicted. Going bankrupt was just unthinkable. I had to make all my bills right. I spent quite a bit of time in prayer about how to do that.

A friend who owned a color lab in Northern Iowa came to visit. Together, we came up with the idea that would be a win for both of us. I owned a printer free and clear. My friend offered to take the printer in exchange for providing a specific dollar amount of color photographic services.

That meant I didn't have to pay any money to get the color prints I needed to stay in business. This extra margin helped me pay off some remaining bills. It was hard to face because I had come full circle. When I started as a photographer, I purchased my color prints from the lab. Then I became a lab owner that sold color prints to other photographers. Because my lab shut down, I again needed to buy prints from a photo lab. By praying for God's help, the deal I struck with my friend saved my business and kept me from going bankrupt.

God sent another well-known photographer friend to me from Northern Iowa. He came on a Monday evening shortly before my studio closed for the evening. There were employees in the studio, so he invited me outside to talk. This brother was a Christ-follower, and I have no idea what we talked about other than we glorified our Savior and praised Him. We talked, and we prayed about my financial situation. Then there was peace, total peace. I knew in my heart that God was in control and would lead me through this financial valley. It took eight years to make a profit again. By then, I had been in business for 25 years. I sensed God was calling me into something new that would honor him.

Bottom Line: I had no control over the decision to close the color lab, but God sent me two people to confirm that decision and provide a financial solution that honored Him. When you have a significant decision to make, involve trusted godly counselors in your life to ensure you are making the right decision.

Ted Hains Shares a Story: Almost Broke— Seeing God Provide

I sold my 25-year-old photography studio on December 30, 1979. So many things were changing all around me. President Reagan was taking over from President Carter, I didn't have a job, and we were considering a photographing adventure from an overseas mission organization. When we said yes to the mission organization, we got a rejection letter. Now what?

I went on a mission trip across the border of Mexico with a friend, taking pictures/slides throughout the journey. When I returned to the US, I put together a two-projector slide presentation with narration by tape. Our church was having a mission conference, and I asked if I could show my slides. They agreed. As it happened, the head of the mission's department from an Evangelical church group was at this conference. He asked me to join their staff because my skills matched what they needed. A week later, I was interviewed by the mission board for the job. My wife, Elaine, and I were accepted and pronounced missionary candidates. We took missionary training and learned that we would be assigned to live in Venezuela for one year, photographing all the missionary ministries there.

I was so thrilled I could hardly contain myself. I had almost three months to wait until we would go. In the meantime, I needed to make some money to support my family. My best friend George came to the rescue. He and I had photographed many weddings together. By trade, he was an interior decorator and did a lot of painting, so he taught me to paint. I now had a new skill, and I was getting paid. It was a real blessing at just the right time, and I loved the work.

Bottom Line: God loves it when we get to the end of our rope. When we get there, we are finally willing to grab on to His rope. In the interim, God had a plan for me. His plan provided for Elaine and me, as well as our whole family. It just wasn't my plan, but God's plan was better! Are you running your plan today or God's?

Chapter 7 Questions

1. The steps in the iWork4Him Nation Covenant came to me through daily practice in my work. The Holy Spirit inspired these steps. There is no other way to explain the change you see when you put them into action. Are you willing to start praying today for those you work alongside every day?

2. We need to have friendships with those we work with, not just a work friendship but a real friendship based on something other than the commonality of work. Relationships take time and effort, but if we are going to transform our workplace into a mission field, relationships are necessary. Jesus got to know people quickly. We need to do the same. Who can you develop a healthy friendship with today?

3. Praying with people when you notice them having a
   hard day? Praying with people may seem daunting.
   However, if your co-worker, boss, or employee just
   shared something painful from their heart, they will
   be open to prayer. I have never had anyone turn me
   down.

4. Ted shares how God brought men into his life to help
   him honor God in his decision to close the color lab.
   Right decisions can be challenging, but God will help
   us make those right decisions if we give Him a
   chance to get involved in our work. God did this
   with Ted. How has He done it with you?

8

Who Do You Work for, Really? iWork4Him

IWORK4HIM IS A revolution based on a revelation. Not a new revelation but one given to us at the beginning of time.

The Revelation

- Our work was given to us by God as a gift.

- God gave us work to bring flourishing to our relationship with Him.

- God intended work to be done together— God and us.

- Work brings satisfaction and accomplishment.

- God intended our work to build our relationship with Him and between us and others.

- Work is a tool of righteousness to point others to Him.

Imagine the United States of America today if all 55 million workplace missionaries understood this revelation. How would this impact our country?

There are roughly one million Christian religious workers in the USA, mostly working inside the church's four walls. The vocational church worker's job is to support and equip (Eph. 4:11-12) the 55 million workplace believers for their ministry at work. Jesus intended the four-walls church to be a manufacturing plant, producing Christ-following workers for every job on the planet. When equipped, these workers will unleash Truth, hope, and life-change at work.

In the past, we expected the Christian religious workers to complete the great commission while we funded them. We now know that it was a false religious doctrine. We cannot expect full-time Christian workers to accomplish the great commission alone. Our job is to bring the gospel message and our transformation to our workplace. The reformation of our hearts toward our work is the beginning of completing our mission.

The Faith and Work Movement started 2,000 years ago. Jesus died around 30 AD, and within a year or so, Christianity spread throughout Jerusalem, Judea, and Samaria. Paul's persecution started dominating the headlines, and Christ-followers fled the oppression, which distributed them throughout the Roman Empire. Once Christ-followers spread throughout the empire, Christianity exploded and millions came to know Jesus as their Savior and Lord. The persecution of Christians also increased during this time, as the worship of Jesus threatened the emperor's worship. The emperor murdered Christ-followers by the thousands.

To better understand what the Bible is saying, it helps to look at the historical and cultural context. Behind the scenes written by Luke in the book of Acts, Christianity was spreading rapidly, but how? We know the Holy Spirit moved in radical day-long events like Pentecost, but what happened on the other days? Wherever Jesus-followers went, they had to work. In their work, they also shared about Jesus. In the marketplace, word spread fast, so news of Jesus spread quickly too. All over the Roman Empire, slaves, the free, the ruling class, and foreigners heard about Jesus.

It is so important that we realize that they were not just hearing about Jesus on Sunday. They heard about Jesus every day of the week. The people of the Roman Empire noticed something amazingly different about the people who followed Jesus. Their faith was vibrant, and they were willing to die for it. The faith of those following Jesus touched the people they worked alongside and eventually changed the Roman Empire. This pattern of sharing Jesus through work and community relationships continued through the centuries. It is why you know about Jesus today.

Now, back to the USA. What would it be like if all 55 million workplace Jesus-followers became like the early followers of Jesus 2,000 years ago? The vibrancy and authenticity of the Jesus-followers in the Roman Empire transformed the world. That same vibrancy is available to us today, and the Holy Spirit supplies it.

Our vibrancy of faith also comes from understanding God's plan for our work. When 55 million Jesus-followers in our nation embrace their workplace mission field, a wave of healing and hope will cover this land. By plugging into one of the many Faith and Work discipleship ministries, you will be strengthened and encouraged as you learn to embrace your workplace mission field.

Everything about us started changing the moment we became followers of Jesus. For some, miraculous change happened immediately. For all of us, there is a lifetime of the refining fire ahead. The refining in your heart and mind is miraculous, and others can witness it when we make it visible. The unlimited power of change comes from God through the Holy Spirit.

Imagine your life with a faith that applies to everything you do, not just on Sunday but every day. Imagine a faith that impacts you so completely that your life radiates Jesus in all that you do. Whether you are digging a ditch, running for office, starting a company, teaching a student, or cooking a meal, your work matters to God. When you build a building, organize a political campaign, or run cable lines, your work involves people. Imagine your faith in Jesus impacting every personal interaction in your work.

Faith in Jesus is:

- Faith that propels you to operate in obedience to God's Word

- Faith that propels you to love your neighbor as yourself

- Faith that loves the least of these as Jesus described in Matthew 25:40-45

- Faith that gives you a purpose and reason for living

Faith like this changed the world 2,000 years ago. Faith like this will change our world today. Our country needs you to live out your faith at work.

Coming to a biblical understanding of my work caused me to live with a ton of regret. I was devastated because:

- I had 20 years in the marketplace where my work behavior did not match my behavior on Sunday.

- I had missed so many ministry opportunities in my work with customers, vendors, and employees.

- I did not have a godly workplace believer investing in my life.

- I had been misguided by many Christians about my work's significance, even though I wasn't a pastor or missionary.

This regret could have left me crippled and defeated, but God challenged me to repent and change. I apologized to many people and continued to learn more about what Scripture says about my work. You don't have to live with regret. Take time now to seek forgiveness, repent, and start fresh.

When I realized the call on my life was to be in ministry wherever I found myself, I gained such peace. God is involved in my work, so I am never alone. When the 330 million people of the United States see Jesus-followers living out this kind of faith at work, many will meet Jesus for the first time.

iWork4Him is a statement of faith. It is not a club that you join. It is a recognition of the reality of your work situation. Your workplace is your mission field, so you can ultimately say, "iWork4Him. "

www.iWork4Him.com can be your starting place to access thousands of faith and work-related podcasts, weekly blogs, and connections to other ministries. Please use it as the resource to help you on your way to living out your faith in your work.

Remember my quote from the beginning of our show: "The job that you hold, the work that you do, the people that you work with—none of that is by chance. The people that you work with need to meet Jesus, and you may be their only chance."

Have fun and make sure to share your stories with us at:

- Jim@iWork4Him.com
- Martha@iWork4Him.com

Ted Hains Shares a Story: Almost Broke—Learning to Say Yes, Not **Never**

Three months of painting had passed quickly. Now I was finally going to start moving forward on our plan to move to the mission field. I went to Minneapolis, Minnesota for missionary orientation. Our two youngest girls stayed home in Illinois to finish their school year, knowing that they would be at Christensen Academy in Rubio, Venezuela, the next school year.

We spent the next few months traveling to different churches to raise money for our mission support. Our girls, Mary and Martha, would play the piano and sing, and we explained how our work would make it easier for missionaries to tell the story of their mission work in Venezuela. We would be photographing the missionaries on location and providing them with beautiful slides of their mission work right from their native mission field. We were able to raise enough money to go on our one-year mission. Much of this money came from our friends and family.

We had a fantastic year in Venezuela. Our daughters loved their school in the village of Rubio. Elaine and I went to visit them during Thanksgiving break.

The director of the school took me on a guided tour around the facility. He stopped by a path that led west and said, "That path leads to Cucuta, Colombia."

"Cucuta?" I repeated.

Memories came flooding back. I had been on a mission trip to Colombia before our two girls were born almost 20 years prior. When I was on that mission trip, I prayed, "Lord use my skills to serve you, but don't send me to a place like this." I laughed out loud! The Lord has such a sense of humor! I could not get any closer to Cucuta and not be there than I was at that moment.

After a year, our time in Venezuela came to an end. We made a lot of friends and helped a lot of missionaries. There was a sadness about leaving, as I could see that an awful lot of work still needed to be done if this country were ever to become centered on Christ.

Bottom Line: Often, we like to tell God what we will and will not do. That is one of the worst ideas ever. When we surrender our lives to Jesus, we need to learn to be obedient to the Lord our God. He knows what is best and often likes to put our stubbornness in front of us to learn from it. What have you told the Lord that you would "never" go or do? Ask forgiveness and respond to our Heavenly Father with these words, "Not my will, but yours be done."

Ted Hains Shares a Story: Almost Broke—Adversity

When our family came back off the mission field in Venezuela, we moved to Minneapolis. My job was now working in the mission's department of our church's denomination. I set up a photo studio and made prayer cards for each missionary. There was no end to the potential for mission uses of photography.

One day the president of the denomination came to see me. "Teddy," he said, "our denomination is about to have its one-hundredth anniversary, and I want you to make an eight-projector sound production that will make me proud. I want you to transfer from the mission department to the denomination headquarters."

"But, sir, I feel God called me into missions," I said.

"Well, if you ever expect to earn more money …."

I knew I had a dilemma, so I asked my pastor if we could have lunch. I remember him telling me, "You need to be submissive to those in authority over you." The next day I told the president I would transfer. The 100th anniversary came and went; the slide presentation was a big hit. And everybody was congratulating everyone over the success the convention had been.

About a month later, it was my turn to lead chapel. I wanted to share Jeremiah 29:11, so I had the print shop print some five by seven cards with the verse "'For I know the plans I have for you,' declares the Lord, 'plans to prosper you and not to harm you, plans to give you hope and a future'" (NIV). Everyone in attendance received one. After the meeting, the business manager told me he wanted me to meet with him and the president in the boardroom at 3 p.m.

At the meeting, the president and finance director said the finances in the denomination had dropped and they were going to have to let some people go. And I was the first.

It was Thanksgiving time. I requested a hearing, including the director of missions from whom I had always gotten praise but never a review. The day came. I reminded them that most of my salary came from my mission support.

The president looked at the business manager and said, "Is that true?"

It was, but it didn't matter. I then asked the director of missions if I could return to my old job. I said, "If you needed me then, perhaps you could use me now?"

He replied, "Maybe we didn't need you then."

I was shocked. They gave me four months to find a new job. My Bible study group encouraged me to go back into business. I resisted and decided to take a job as a salesman for a local company. I was a salesman for just a year until I decided to go back into the photography business.

I learned a lot of lessons. Some of which made me very sarcastic. Most of them hurt deeply, but I decided to take the high road and move on. Telling this story almost four decades later, I'm still sad because I loved what I was doing to support mission work around the globe but, as God knew better than me, mission work was changing, and today there is no need for missionary slide shows.

God also knew that he had gifted me with incredible photography skills and the ability to be an entrepreneur. In the 13 years after getting fired, Elaine and I grew a thriving business. We not only recovered from being almost broke, but we were also able to sell our business before we were 70, and it has provided for our mission work in our retirement years. God is so good. He knew better than me from the beginning. I know God called me to missions, and I am doing missions today every time I share the Gospel of John with someone who has never seen the Bible.

Bottom Line: Often, we see terrible adversity as a negative, and we argue and complain to God and ask Him to rescue us from it. God used the adversity of us closing our business in Illinois, the time in Venezuela, and our move to MPLS to put a ton of healing in place for our lives. He had a bigger plan. I learned to trust Him through it all. What about you? Do you fight God in adversity? I learned God always uses the adversity in our lives to take us from who we are to who He can use more effectively. Whatever draws us closer to Him is a *win*.

Chapter 8 Questions

1. Who do you work for, really?

2. Imagine our country with 55 million Christ-followers who are active in their faith and recognize their work as their primary place of ministry outside of their home. How would this transform our country?

3. Ted shares how God used an apparent financial disaster to move him from his Illinois mission field to Venezuela and then to Minnesota. In Minnesota, God led him to restart his business. His business exploded. The whole family is transformed because Ted took bold steps with his wife, Elaine, by his side. Can you look back and see how God used a disaster in your life to bring you to a whole new level of success?

Part II

THE FOLLOWING PAGES contain notes and information from ministries throughout the Faith and Work Movement. We asked them to contribute to this book for three reasons:

1. Awareness – That you would be aware of their presence in the Faith and Work Movement.

2. Encouragement – To encourage you by hearing how they disciple the everyday worker to live out their faith in their work.

3. Connection – To make a connection with the ministries that resonate with your heart.

These contributors are friends and co-laborers in the Kingdom of God. We honor them in this collaborative effort because the Kingdom is about The One.

Enjoy.

9

Note from Os Hillman

Marketplace Leaders

MARKETPLACE LEADERS WAS founded in 1994 after Os Hill-man, a former advertising agency owner for 12 years, went through a seven-year personal crisis that led to the birthing of Marketplace Leaders. Os began to realize that many men and women in the workplace struggle to integrate their faith life into their work life. He also realized that the failure to do this was leaving a vacuum in the culture, allowing anti-God philosophies to undermine our Christian cultural foundations.

He committed to sharing what he had learned from his adversity experiences. This focus led Os to write 21 books and speak and train leaders in 26 countries worldwide. Os became a recognized leader and authority in the Faith and Work Movement globally, appearing on CNBC and ABC, and in the *New York Times* and *LA Times*. Peter Wagner cited Os as "arguably the most knowledgeable leader on the topic of faith in work in the world today."

Os realized that culture is often shaped by leaders who operate at the upper levels in business, government, media, arts and entertainment, education, government, and religion. It only took a small portion of 3 to 5% of leadership to impact the culture. Os decided that this concept must be part of the Marketplace Leaders strategy and subsequently incorporated it into the ministry.

84% of Christian 18 to 29-year-olds admit that they have no idea how the Bible applies to their field or professional interests.
—Barna Group,June, 2012.

We sense that our nation has been given a window of opportunity to reclaim some of its faith foundations lost during previous administrations. There is much dysfunction in our political system, and the level of the national debt is a major dark cloud over the nation and is subject to a major financial crisis at any time. Marketplace Leaders desire to affect the leadership in our country and other nations to help reestablish faith foundations where opportunities exist.

- *Our Vision:* Transform leaders to transform culture.

- *Our Mission:* Marketplace Leaders is a voice and agent to inspire, teach, and connect Christian believers to resources and relationships in order to manifest the life of Christ in their workplace call for cultural influence.

The Three Primary Goals of Marketplace Leaders Are to:

1. Raise awareness of the need to integrate faith and work in the lives of Christian workplace believers.

2. Identify, attract, and train change agents for restoring biblical foundations within our nation and the world.

3. Convene and mobilize change agents to transform society to reflect Christian principles and values.

The Problem

For the last 50 years, America has been moving away from the spiritual foundations that made it a great nation. *A Pew Research report in May of 2015 revealed a drop by 7% of those who claim Christianity as their faith, and* our research shows that our nation is in jeopardy of losing its leadership position in the world because of a fractured spiritual foundation.

The statistic in this graphic reveals the problem we have in our nation. Young Americans have lost their understanding of how their spiritual life connects with their work-life call. Since 300 AD, culture has segmented faith life from work life. It was during this time culture began to propose a dualism in work and ministry. This has led to a moral vacuum in our nation as leaders isolated themselves from spiritual values in the workplace. As individuals moved away from God, ungodly leadership began to allow ungodly values to be incorporated into our culture. We have become the proverbial frog in the kettle over the last 50 years, not realizing our deteriorating values that are moving us away from our spiritual foundations as a nation.

Strategy

Marketplace Leaders will accomplish its mission by serving individuals within our three core audiences through our vast armory of teaching and training tools.

Our Three Core Audiences

As we are called to serve Christian leaders in all stages of life, Marketplace Leaders focuses on the following core audiences:

1. *Workplace leaders* – We help *all* workplace leaders better understand the spiritual nature and the potential Kingdom impact of their work-life call.

2. *"Josephs"* – We serve those whom God has placed in the crucible of extremely difficult circumstances and help them navigate through this tumultuous season of life and move into their distinct calling.

3. *Culture-shapers* – We serve those God has placed at the top tiers of leadership within the seven cultural mountains.

Our 3 Core Audiences

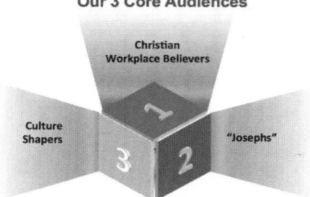

Core Products and Services

The following are the core services we provide to fulfill our above vision and mission.

Today God Is First: Daily Workplace Inspiration by Os Hillman

Our initial engagement process with our audiences often involves the reading of TGIF, Today God Is First, a daily email devotional written by our founder, Os Hillman, read by several hundred thousand people daily. In 2018, we distributed over 54 million TGIF messages to 104 countries. Actual readership is estimated at two to three times this amount through multiple media platforms and pass-alongs by subscribers to others in their circle of relationships. Subscribe at www.TodayGodIsFirst.com.

Journey to Your Destiny: Change Agent Master Mentor Program

The Change Agent MasterMentor program is an online equipping website that features 35 courses and 141 sessions plus 250 podcast interviews, 54 video case studies, and a mentoring call and prayer call once a month. Learn more at www.CAMasterMentor.com

TGIF@Work with OsHillman

Every Thursday, we produce a TGIF@Work podcast featured on iTunes and YouTube.

- www.YouTube.com/oshillman
- iTunes: Os Hillman TGIF
- podcasts.apple.com/us/podcast/tgif-today-god-is-first-by-os-hillman/id367599244

International Culture Shapers Summit

In 2019, we hosted the International Culture Shapers Summit. You can find over 50 presentations on our website at www.CultureShapersSummit.com.

Os Hillman
Founder of Marketplace
Leaders

www.TodayGodIsFirst.com
www.MarketplaceLeaders.org
www.CAMasterMentor.com

iWork4Him Podcast

- http://bit.ly/2JTI1fK

10

Note from Doug Spada

*WorkLife: Why Is Your Life
at Work so Important?*

IF YOU'RE LIKE MOST people, you spend 90,000 hours of your life working. And how you work influences every other aspect of your life, such as your time, talent, treasure, and family.

God is definitely interested in your work! Yet many of us really don't know how to enjoy more of God's power in our work. If we are honest, many of us are not even sure work has anything to do with God.

How about you? Do you ever treat your work as if it were unrelated to God? Without much thought, many of us label what we perceive to be the unspiritual segments of life as "secular." Did you know that the word secular means "without God"? Here is the problem with that. There is no place on this planet where God does not function. We are designed to not just do missions, like a mission trip—we are designed to be on mission every day, no matter what our particular job might be. In short, real biblical ministry is done by God's people wherever he has put them or wherever they find themselves. Listen to this amazing encouragement from the Bible:

> So here's what I want you to do, God helping you: Take your everyday, ordinary life—your sleeping, eating, going—to—work, and walking around life—and place it before God as an offering. (Rom. 12:1 MSG)

God created you with your attributes, your unique DNA! You did not select your attributes any more than you chose your eye color. Your gifts and talents are no more or less valuable than the next person, no matter their spiritual status or your role at work. You only get to choose what you are going to do with your talents. The key to real success at work has little to do with what job you have or what talents you have—it has much more to do with choosing God first and doing the best you can. Your real job is to use your God-given gifts to the best of your ability, right where you are.

God desires to help you and bless you as you work. He wants you to thrive. Do not settle for less than that for which you were made. You are created uniquely to do special work in God's eyes.

Testimonies

> Helen: I can't tell you what a difference this is making in my personal relationship with Christ. My faith is becoming real to me, 24/7.

Rachel: I am experiencing so much more joy and more peace. Before this kind of help, my faith was lacking, and I could not sense God's presence and help at work, or really anywhere else. I am so much more aware of Him working in all of my life.

Chris: I have never had joy and courage like I do now. I am praying for my co-workers, and even had a conversation about Christ with my boss, our company CEO. I am so happy and full of joy. Before this kind of help, this area of my life was mostly untouched by God's presence.

Doug's Personal Story

Many years ago, I experienced a personal crisis. God had little involvement in my work life, and as a result, I let my work and character collapse. My success was superficial, my spiritual life was in shambles, and I watched my family slip through my fingers. God restored my family, but I had to look at work and life in a completely different way. This journey eventually led me to found WorkLife.

WorkLife Today

WorkLife seeks to awaken and engage Christians in the marketplace to live God-infused, spirit-directed, joy-filled work lives—to better thrive in work and life. To do this, we recognize an alarming spiritual pandemic in our culture and around the world.

Nearly three billion people enter the workplace every week spiritually asleep on the job. They work in politics, business, education, entertainment, and more. After years of research, WorkLife has found that most suffer from *Monday Morning Atheism.* We call this collective group of people *The Sleeping Giant.*

Monday Morning Atheism

A Monday Morning Atheist is someone who loves God but works like He does not exist. As a result, Christ is less visible in our culture, and we continue to lose the spiritual battle. And if we are honest, we can see that we all suffer from some degree of Monday Morning Atheism from time to time.

Awakening the Sleeping Giant

WorkLife is now leading a global campaign called *Awaken the Sleeping Giant.* This global campaign inspires and equips working believers at their greatest point of ministry and service, their work.

It includes a multiyear creative communications effort through national media channels to Awaken the Sleeping Giant (Christians) in America. This effort is a biblically inspired call to action for workers of every vocation to Switch God ON (to live and work in ways that amplify the presence of our God on Monday). It is provocative but uses a very practical process to eradicate the epidemic of Monday Morning Atheism in Christians.

This effort results in empowered Christians transforming their community (business, church, city, family, politics, etc.) in critical areas of time, talent, and treasure. This is an amazing opportunity to advance Christian values and beliefs.

Today, WorkLife serves individual workers, churches, businesses, and organizations around the world.

WorkLife resources include the following books:

- *Monday Morning Atheist*
- *The Switch: 6 Steps to God's Power at Work*

There are also numerous additional WorkLife tools, assessments, and other products on our website—many of them free.

Doug Spada
Founder, WorkLife

www.Worklife.org

iWork4Him Podcast

- http://bit.ly/3hP1dYp

11

Note from David J. Collum

The Pocket Testament League

BALANCE. WE LIVE AT a place and in a time when all of us expect we can live balanced, fulfilling lives. We hope balance is within our grasp.

So we listen to those who are pursuing this dream, yet it eludes us. Our response is not to give up. We keep looking and listening. We find more people, those who seemingly have achieved this elusive balance here on earth. We then pursue it with even more vigor, seeking more advice and input. Yet our effort backfires.

The increased information reinforces how far we must go. Our demand has created a din of daily messages regarding pursuing our passion, finding our purpose, or becoming people of peace. This pressure to pursue and possess is pervasive. Our reaction? We now redouble our efforts with exponentially increasing expectations.

How can I make such an assertion? Simple. The market. Consider that when most printed material is being devastated by the digital world, books in the genre of self-improvement are predicted to grow to $13.2 billion by 2022. Imagine if we were to add to this in-print market the blogs, e-books, etc. It seems as if we are screaming for help.

Satisfying this human desire is not a new endeavor. Greek philosophers wrestled with what true human flourishing looked like for centuries. They came up with a variety of answers.

So why then would I add to this mountain of material? Because I believe the way forward is rooted not in new learning but in eternal truth. This truth provides both a solid foundation and daily practicum. This eternal truth is found in the Bible—at its beginning, in Genesis.

In God's Word, we find our purpose. *We find it not in statement but in story.* God created all, and it was very good. His crowning creation was humankind, and He made us in his image—male and female. In this world, God walked in the garden in the cool of the evening, seeking fellowship with Adam and Eve.

We are created to be with God and live for God, not as robots or servants but as His friends and stewards of His creation. It seems each generation finds itself searching for this reality. When they find it, they express it in the language of their day. One generation described it this way: "The chief end of mankind is to glorify God and enjoy him forever."

"Glorifying and enjoying God forever" sounds terribly religious. It was their generation's way of taking hold of this biblical truth and explaining it. Notice the grammar. Our chief end, or you might say aim, is in the present grammatical tense. This manner of living is now and is meant never to end.

You might be thinking, "I can't believe you are laying religion and Bible on me. I have real-world pressure." I get your situation. I have that same one. I would ask you to consider this question: What if you could focus everything in your life—your marriage, your family, your career, and your pleasures—through a single unifying lens? Would having such a lens order the fragmented pieces of your world?

It would for me. Consider a single unifying focus, the person of Jesus. The God of creation come to earth for you. If you are reading this, I will assume you know Jesus. I expect you may have asked Jesus into your heart. Perhaps you attend church, yet I want to ask, are you still seeking this flourishing life?

Unifying your life in and through the person of Jesus is the answer to having a flourishing life, yet Jesus is not some tool we acquire for our end. Loving Jesus is our response to God's love for us. When we do so, we naturally give God glory.

What happens is we stop pursuing life for some goal that, at best, is distorted. Instead, we live for Jesus. We live to know and love Him. The challenge with phrases such as "living for Jesus" is they sound religious. Those words lack how to do it.

Countless books have been authored on spiritual practices. I want to suggest three daily steps to stay with Him. If you miss doing them one day, it wouldn't be the end of the world. Just start anew the next day.

Step One: Be with Jesus by reading His Word. I don't care how much you read. I care *how* you read. Read conversationally (some call it devotionally). Let me give an example. Psalm 34:8 reads, "Taste and see that the Lord is good"

(NLT). I suggest you pause and ask yourself, ask Jesus, "How can I taste you, Lord?" You might be amazed at the answers. You might then pray. This type of reading is not trying to read the Bible in a year. Look, I've done that. It's cool. But I suggest you set a time goal to sit with God's Word. Do this each day.

Step Two: Carry God's Word with you to *share* with another. At the Pocket Testament League (www.PTL.org), you can obtain pocket-sized Gospels of John with a variety of attractive covers. As you prepare for your day, picking up your car keys, or wallet, or purse—pick up a Gospel of John and pray, "Lord, lead me to the person you want me to give this to today. You might be thinking, "This is screwy." I know, but let's get to Step Three.

Step Three: God is going to prompt you to give that Gospel to a person. And you, well, you will feel anxious, maybe even have a little fear. If you ask God for help, you will offer this Gospel with kindness and without argument. And here is what you will learn. Every day, you must give Jesus away. He is not someone for you to keep to yourself. When you give Him away, you are in a very practical way acknowledging to yourself, to Him, and the world that He is the truth that not simply unified your life. He has saved you.

This last practical step is powerful. People in the 12-Step program know it. You have to give it away to keep it. It is not that you become what many picture as an evangelist with all sorts of rhetorical expertise. No, you are merely a fellow sojourner on this planet who realized the need to be saved, and Jesus found you. You simply want to invite others to consider letting Him save them as well.

If you faithfully do these three simple steps. You will notice the fragments of your life coming into focus. It will happen miraculously.

David J. Collum
President and Chief Executive Officer of The Pocket Testament League

www.PTL.org

iWork4Him Podcast

- http://bit.ly/3pZtezk
- http://bit.ly/35mSjwj

12

Note from the Theology
of Work Project

THE THEOLOGY OF WORK (TOW) Project is the deepest, largest, and most trusted source of biblical, theological, and pastoral material related to work. The TOW Project resources are meant to be both theologically rigorous and genuinely practical. Most TOW materials are available free of charge at www.TheologyofWork.org.

The TOW Project is committed to bringing the Bible into the real-life experience of work in every sphere of society. The Bible has an incredible wealth of counsel. Nearly 900 passages apply to ordinary work. TOW materials on topics such as calling, conflict at work, performance, ethics, finance, fear of failure, difficult bosses, rest, truth, and deception, and changing jobs have been used by millions of individuals and small groups. Leading figures in the Faith and Work Movement endorse and use TOW resources.

TOW's cornerstone resource, the *Theology of Work Bible Commentary*, is the only commentary covering what the entire Bible says about work. It is available for free in its entirety at www.TheologyofWork.org. The *Theology of Work*

Bible Commentary can be accessed in English, Spanish, Korean, and Chinese.

The TOW Project is providing desperately needed resources to pastors and the entire church on what the Bible has to say about our work (Tim Keller, pastor, Redeemer Church).

This commentary was written exactly for those of us who aim to integrate our faith and work on a daily basis and is an excellent reminder that God hasn't called the world to go to church but has called the Church to go to the world (Bonnie Wurzbacher, former senior vice president, The Coca-Cola Company).

Other popular resources include:

The *Making It Work* podcast (www.MakingIt-Workpodcast.org) is produced in partnership with Fuller Seminary's De Pree Center for leadership. Making *It Work* helps listeners invite God into their biggest work-related challenges through Scripture, conversation, and story.

I am so appreciative of this podcast; I listen to it on the way to work. It has prepared my heart for the day, reminded me of ways I can bring spiritual discipline into work and provided counsel before important meetings—thank you. —Making It Work podcast listener

Devotional reading plans on the YouVersion Bible App (www.TheologyofWork.org/devotions), such as *How to Make the Right Decision, Anxiety About Money, Working through Failure,* and more.

I cannot tell you how much this devotional has blessed me. I am eager every morning to read it and get more wisdom as well as to calm my anxiety. —*Devotional reading plan reader*

Calling and Vocation Overview (www.TheologyofWork.org/key-topics/vocation-overview-article)

Small group studies (https://www.TheologyofWork.org/small-group-studies)

The vision of the Theology of Work Project is that every Christian be equipped and committed to work as God intends. A Christian approach makes work more meaningful and productive, benefits society and the people we work with and for, gets us through the challenges we face on the job, draws people to Jesus, and brings glory to God.

Theology of Work
www.TheologyofWork.org

iWork4Him Podcast (Will Messenger)

- http://bit.ly/3np4Dm2

iWork4Him Podcast (Faith and Work Bible)

- https://bit.ly/2XmfFh6

iWork4Him Podcast (Leah Archibald)

- http://bit.ly/2LscTo7

13

Note from T.J. Tison

Working Women of Faith:
Killing Wonder Woman

EVERY WOMAN IS A working woman, whether that work takes place in the home or outside of the home. It's all hard work. Yet there are special challenges for women of faith who work outside the home. There is so much to do and so little time. We often feel pulled in a million directions. We may know that God has equipped us for the work He has called us to do. We may know He has called us to care for our homes and families, but how can we do both well? And how do we find space to pursue our relationship with Jesus in the midst of all our "to-dos? We not only feel pulled in a million directions externally, but we also feel pulled internally as well. Our workplace rarely supports our pursuit of faith, and sadly, our faith communities rarely support our pursuit of work.

To succeed, we feel like we need to be Wonder Woman to achieve the perfect work-life balance. But we all know the truth—Wonder Woman isn't real.

If it's true that we can never be her, what is the solution?

Working Women of Faith: Killing Wonder Woman

Let's start with the Working Women of Faith, a place for women to "get real" about their work, life, and faith. It's a place for women to learn to integrate faith into all aspects of their lives, especially the workplace. This membership-based community provides practical, biblical-based teaching relevant to working women today. Through monthly meetings, authentic conversations with women of faith, and resources, women learn to grow in the knowledge of who God has built them to be, not who the world expects them to be.

Working Women of Faith is a respite, a chance to hit the pause button and connect with God, themselves, and others on neutral ground. It is a time to put away the to-do list and start with who is doing the to-do list and who has called us to the to-do list.

We cover topics like shame, success, failure, and integrating our faith in our callings. At our meetings, women find a place for real talk—a struggle with a boss, a fight with a teenager, or managing care for an aging parent while balancing a full-time job.

Working Women of Faith uses a chapter model that allows for groups to be led by women of the community to be launched in any community. Not only do we provide chapter leaders with the tools and support to start a chapter, but we also provide the leadership training to equip them to lead other women to integrate their faith in life and work. Additionally, we pay our chapter leaders a percentage of their chapter membership fees. We believe women volunteer enough and deserve to get paid for their time.

Working Women of Faith was created by T.J. Tison. T.J. saw the need for community and resources within the faith community that at that time had been unavailable matched with her desire to run her own business as a ministry on a mission field. Women of faith know that their work matters to God just as much as their role as a wife and parent. Everyone needs wisdom and guidance to build a business God's way, share Jesus through calling, and create an eternal impact in the world beyond the four walls of their home and church. So as many things begin, Working Women of Faith was not only created to fill a void but to build a purpose.

So what about Killing Wonder Woman?

Killing Wonder Woman: Setting Weary Women Free to Win at Work and Soar in Faith is more than a book; it's a field guide for every woman, but especially for Working Women of Faith. This book and the corresponding digital class and workbook are given to each member when they register. This is crucial training for Working Women of Faith. It helps them recognize the "Wonder Woman lies" and their true source—from across enemy lines.

The curriculum explores the need to be set free and replacing those lies with God's truth. Once free, women are ready to explore how to win at work by seeing their work as a ministry and mission field while learning to navigate the minefields that are eventual in our work/faith integration. Lastly, women are taken through key components to soaring to new levels in their faith-walk. Killing Wonder

Woman is the key to living the abundant life without the heavy burdens we as women bear.

Killing Wonder Woman: Setting Weary Women Free to Win at Work and Soar in Faith was written to answer the lack of resources for women of faith in the workplace to fulfill a great purpose.

For more information about Working Women of Faith and *Killing Wonder Woman,* visit workingwomenoffaith.com. There you will find information on how to become a member, member benefits, and how to start a chapter in your area. You can also purchase the *Killing Wonder Woman* book and class in the Working Women of Faith store.

TJ Tison
Co-owner and Educational Engineer for the E5 Institute, founder of Working Women of Faith

WorkingWomenofFaith.com

iWork4Him Podcast

- http://bit.ly/3pYBvnb

14

Note from Mike Henry
and Jessica Fletcher

Marketplace Missions Trips

FOLLOWER OF ONE IS an online community for marketplace Christ-followers who want their work life to count for eternity.

Mike's Story

Shortly after we launched Follower of One, I was having coffee with a friend and recalled how, years earlier, I asked my pastor how I could help him. He said we needed more people to go on an upcoming Mexico mission trip. He said when people come back from a mission trip, they come back on fire for Jesus. His eyes lit up as he said, "They got it!"

I responded to my pastor that I felt like I already "got it," and I drove 30 miles one way daily to work. I then asked, "How is that not a mission trip?"

This conversation with my pastor didn't go much further. But as I told this story to my friend, he quickly said, "Why don't you organize a virtual mission trip?"

My mind began to race. I immediately started thinking about how we could create a "virtual" mission trip. The more we thought about it, the easier it seemed. I came away from that coffee meeting with new energy. How could I create a virtual mission trip for every believer?

A mission trip typically involves a week or two of travel to some faraway place to work and get to know the local people. These short-term missionaries hope to share Christ, but they will still help people out if nothing else.

Why couldn't we encourage people to go to their job the same way they would go on a mission trip?

Jessica's Story

I led a Bible study group for singles and couples between the ages of 25 and 40. One of the most common discussions we would have during the group was how to build our faith in the places we feel the weakest. Almost unanimously, each time, everyone seemed to voice that work, and their workplaces, were the areas that we struggled to share and live out our faith. Each person could relate to feelings of lack of direction in displaying their faith in places where it might be considered taboo or counter to their workplace cultures to be open and share their faith.

At times, we may feel it easier than other times to share our faith at work, but we often don't view our work as a place where talking about Christ may be acceptable or even necessary. We go to work, do our job, and go home. That's about it. Some days we have delays or interruptions—an accident on the highway making you late or spilling coffee on your shirt as you walk in the door. For the most part, though, work is just that—it's work.

What if work wasn't just work but a place that we go to every day with the purpose of something more than just doing our job? What if it was your calling? What if it was the one place that God needed you to be? What if there was an entire group of people asking these questions and doing the same thing while praying for you each day intentionally? Would it change the way you do your job? These were questions I started asking myself after Mike brought Follower of One to me.

Mike is my dad, and over family dinner one night, Mike shared Follower of One with me. As he talked about Marketplace Mission Trips, I thought back to all those conversations I had with my Bible study group and knew this met a need. I knew this was the answer for anyone who felt they needed some support in living out their faith at work or strengthening their relationship with Christ at work. I told him to sign me up.

Since joining Follower of One, I have been on several of these mission trips. I am plugged into the community on various social media channels. These tools help me be more intentional about my work for Christ at my job. This may sound like it is difficult, but most of my co-workers don't even know I'm on a mission trip. They may not notice anything at all, but I do. Being more intentional with my workday by following simple steps, praying more, and being accountable to others has completely changed my work and how I view it.

Marketplace Mission Trips

The Marketplace Mission Trips give marketplace Christians a strategy and a plan of action. We lay out five daily activities any Christ-follower can do in any job or situation:

1. Pray
2. Appreciate Others
3. Know What You Believe
4. Serve Others
5. Speak for Yourself

In the first week, we explain each of these activities in detail. In the second week, we encourage you as you put these activities into practice. We also host Zoom video calls to share stories of how God is working too.

In the end, everything comes down to our willingness to act, trusting God. One friend who took the mission trip told a story of traveling to a distant assignment for the week. He and a non-believing co-worker were together on this project, but each one lived miles from each other and this job site. As technology consultants for a large global company, they would probably never see each other again. So our friend followed the Marketplace Mission Trip plan and began praying about what God wanted him to do.

The first seven days, the two had spoken some, and our missionary knew the other person didn't have a relationship with Jesus. By the middle of the second week, he became convicted to give his gospel bracelet to this co-worker. On their last day together, as our missionary prayed and asked God for a way to offer the bracelet, the conversation turned.

As they were about to part at the airport, our missionary offered the bracelet to his co-worker, who accepted. As they were putting it on, the co-worker asked the giver about the significance of the beads. Our missionary then took the opportunity to share the gospel by explaining what each of the various beads represented. He was energized that God had used him to present the gospel, and he was excited having intentionally interacted with Jesus and integrated his faith for the whole two-week period of the trip!

It doesn't have to be a bracelet. God has used a Dr. Pepper, donuts, and a video game to show up in conversations between members of the trip and co-workers. Many take the trip multiple times because they appreciate the experience of walking with Jesus and interacting with others on the trip. Many people enjoy the camaraderie on the Zoom calls and the joy they experience trusting Jesus day by day.

The Marketplace Mission Trip serves as a two-week trial balloon. We hope you become a full-time missionary to your workplace. During the trip, you will learn five daily activities that put you on-mission with Jesus. And you receive daily encouragement by email, podcast, video, and prayer to help you practice those activities in any job situation or workplace.

There's no charge for the trip either. Many people contribute, allowing others to share the experience. Over 250 people have taken at least one of the previous 11 Marketplace Mission Trips at this writing. Imagine what our world looks like when our church friends go on a mission trip to their job every day!

Why not join us on the next one? Head over to MarketplaceMissionTrip.com to learn more and sign up.

Jessica Fletcher
911 Dispatch Supervisor
and Follower of One
Board member

Mike Henry Sr.
Follower of One Founder
and CEO

Websites

- www.FollowerofOne.org

- www.MarketplaceMissionTrip.com

iWork4Him Podcast

- http://bit.ly/3s3P073

15

Note from Catherine Gates

*Workmatters: Pursuing God's
Purpose for Your Work*

*I came to work each day, not completely hiding my
spirituality, but letting it fall into the background.
When I was at work, I brought forth my "work
half." When I received an invitation to participate in
a Christian Employee Resource Group at work, I
was interested yet, at the same time, skeptical. I
learned of Bible studies happening in my workplace.
As I participated, the most noticeable change was
the confidence I had in my core responsibilities and
my identity. I was growing as a confident, more productive employee. Though I have always worked
with great integrity and commitment, this was an
entirely new level. The ability to be completely
whole in the workplace is exponential in power. I
have discovered that no longer having to switch on
and off, the energy and confidence I experience goes
through the roof.*

—Kami, Zurich, N.A.

WORKMATTERS LOVES TO be a catalyst for stories like Kami's. Too many people dread Mondays, feel consumed by their work, and are overwhelmed by stress. Even the most devout Christians struggle under the weight of pressure at work. While work is more complicated today than ever, a significant and overlooked factor of workplace stress is that many of us are doing our work under our own strength. But it doesn't have to be that way.

I get it. It never occurred to me that I could turn to God in my work until I was in my 40s and got to work with Joy in sales at a Long Island company. In our sales meetings, Joy gave glory to God for every sale. She prayed with her customers when they had a need. Joy inspired me to think about what it would look like for me to integrate my faith into my work.

I moved to Arkansas in 2009 and heard David Roth, president of Workmatters, give the Labor Day weekend sermon on the topic of faith and work at the church I was attending. I was so excited to hear that there was an organization that helped people integrate their faith into their work. I started attending the monthly Friday morning breakfast meetings they held at the time. There were over 100 people at that first meeting! Each month a different business leader in the community would share what it looked like for him or her to live out their faith at work, and people would write down their takeaway on a small index card.

I jumped into volunteering at the meetings almost immediately. After less than two years, I was convinced that I would work at Workmatters and told David as much. It was difficult for him to imagine since the organization was still fairly small. But in 2012, God led David to spruce up a workplace Bible study he had written based on the book of Nehemiah. David approached the CEO of the company I was working for about helping him with this project. I was an instructional designer and made sure I was on the writing team. I also volunteered to help David train study facilitators. After just one year, the studies had become so popular that the board of Workmatters recommended hiring someone to oversee this new ministry area. Enter: me.

I joined the team of Workmatters as Director of Workmatters Studies within two years after I had predicted I would, and the Workmatters team continued to grow. We went from serving people in Northwest Arkansas to equipping people all over the world. And Workmatters continues to look for new and more powerful ways to equip greater numbers of Christians in workplaces across the country.

The Workmatters' mission is to help people *close the gap between faith and work — to pursue God's purpose for their work.* Work was given to us as a blessing from the very beginning, and God wants us to turn to Him for strength, insights, and direction for our work. The Workmatters' vision is to equip one million leaders of faith to integrate their faith at work by 2025.

Here are the key ways the team is accomplishing this vision:

Workmatters Conference: Highly respected leaders from across the country gather for the annual Workmatters Conference. Every speaker shares practical insights and tools that equip attendees to grow as leaders and integrate their faith at work.

Attendees are both inspired by the authenticity and vulnerability of the speakers and equipped with proven leadership tools and strategies. The event is 100% spiritual and 100% leadership. Speakers have included executives from Walmart, Facebook, P&G, and Tyson, entrepreneurs, business leaders, speakers, and authors, including Donnie Smith, Doug McMillon, Cheryl Bachelder, Phil Vischer, Nona Jones, Megan Alexander, and Sheeba Philip.

> Having attended many leadership and faith-at-work events across the country, Workmatters Conference has become my all-time favorite conference. The speakers and themes are carefully crafted by the Workmatters team; the event is managed with excellence; the setting encourages deep and meaningful conversations. The result is real life change. (Cheryl Bachelder, Former CEO, Popeyes Louisiana Kitchen, Inc.)

> I was feeling very burnt out and uninspired with my business until I attended Workmatters Conference! I've attended so many conferences, and this one by far gave me more tools and inspiration to move forward with my calling. (Conference attendee)

Workmatters Resources: Workmatters offers small group leadership studies based on biblical principles.

Workmatters Studies help you see biblical stories from a workplace perspective. You can learn from leaders like Nehemiah, Daniel, Esther, and Jesus and gain practical tools to maximize influence, raise the bar on integrity, be more courageous, love people at work, and build workplace community. Every resource is designed to be peer-facilitated—no teacher needed. People going through the studies in a small group of 6 to 12 people (sometimes more) not only learn from the Bible, but they also learn from one another.

On-Demand Learning: For those who prefer video-based studies, subscribers can create a free account and access our on-demand learning modules. Learn from past Workmatters Conference speakers about what it looks like to put biblical principles into practice in their work.

YouVersion Reading Plans: Workmatters has published 14 reading plans on the YouVersion Bible app, including From Crisis to Breakthrough, Leadership Ignited, Give Your Work Meaning, God's Design for Work, and more. (To find all Workmatters reading plans on the YouVersion Bible app, simply go to the Plans, Discover, and search for "Workmatters.")

> The *Maximize Your Influence* study allowed me to see how relevant my daily walk with God was to my work. I was exposed to how Esther showed strength of character, fearlessness, boldness, and resolve, and the power of prayer. These are all qualities we need to help us not only to thrive in the workplace but also in today's society. Now more than ever, I believe that the Bible holds the answer to man's quest for meaning and relevance. (Toyin Umesiri)

Workmatters Institute: At the intersection of theology, leadership, and community, Workmatters Institute is 100% spiritual formation and 100% professional development designed to take early-career professionals on a journey of spiritual and leadership development and application. Workmatters Institute serves everyday people who are eager to address real desires and challenges, serving them in a way that is practical and actionable and reinforces a gospel worldview. Regardless of industry or sphere, embracing God's whole story is the key to conquering the practical challenges of growing a career and growing leaders who have an eternal impact on the world. Every participant develops a Faith and Work Action Plan customized to their needs.

> The sessions/program help prepare you and remind you that God is calling you into the world to restore, rebuild, and let His blessings flow. As you work in the corporate world, Workmatters helps you get firmly established like a tree planted by streams of water to produce good fruit and real impact in your jobs. A real difference-maker. (Jonathan Nimrod, Vice President of Business Development and Sustainability, Shine Electronics, Inc.)

You were created in God's image to do good work, which He prepared for you to do in advance (Ephesians 2:10). God wants to guide you, open doors for you, and bring you success in your work. Workmatters is here to equip you to integrate your faith at work so you can maximize your contribution to bringing His Kingdom to earth.

You can connect with Workmatters by visiting workmatters.org. Our team looks forward to equipping you to pursue God's purpose for your work!

Catherine Gates
Former Senior Director of
Content and Partnerships for
Workmatters, Leadership team
for Christian Women in the
Workplace, Executive Director of
Women in the Marketplace.

www.WorkMatters.org
www.WomeninMarketplace.net

iWork4Him Podcast

- http://bit.ly/3oqclh5

16

Note from Tom and Pam Wolf

Identity and Destiny

"WHY?" THIS IS THE number one question people ask their pastors. Number two? "What's God's purpose for my life?" A mere 3% of people will tell you they know, with certainty, the answer to the second question. The pervasiveness of that question and our own personal search inspired us to go from decades of entrepreneurial business ownership to the work of life purpose discovery.

We are Tom and Pam Wolf. We first created the coaching program, Identity and Destiny—7 Steps to a Purpose-filled Life, and eventually published a workbook outlining the process called *Finding Your God-Given Sweet Spot*. And although God used the two of us to create a program that would transform thousands of lives, we, too, were just as confused as many others about our purpose and calling.

If we were to ask, "Who are you" and "Why are you here"? How would you answer those questions? Likely it would be your title, your role at work or in your family, or the part you play in this great game of life. Is that really who you are? Even more importantly, who does God say you are? After all, He is your Creator, and He created you with a purpose.

> You are God's workmanship, created in Christ Jesus to do good works which God prepared in advance for you to do! (Eph. 2:10)

We spent the first three decades of our working lives building and growing businesses. Like most people, we found our identity and destiny in what we did. Those names are Mom, Dad, Sister, Brother, Business Owner, Leader, and Boss. On the opposite side of that coin, the world slapped some undesirable labels on us. Those labels are a child of a broken home, divorced, remarried, almost bankrupt, or parents of an adult child who died far too young. This list could go on and on.

We found ourselves asking, "How can God use us? With our past mistakes, how can we be worthy of being used by God?" What we found out blew our minds. God knew all about our past and our labels, and He is still head over heels in love with us. God showed us that our mistakes, hard times, and weaknesses make us more usable by the Master. Then He chose us for this incredible assignment of creating Identity and Destiny.

Is this striking a chord? If we ask, "Who are you?" How would you answer? How do you see yourself? What you do, the roles you fill, or the mistakes and bad choices you have made—none of these things define you. God sees you as His one-of-a-kind, handcrafted masterpiece! God sees you with a clear view of your future potential, not through the lens of your past.

To discover your identity is to know who you are at your very core. It is to realize who God has created you to be in this world, regardless of what you do. Your destiny is how the Holy Spirit wants to work in this world through you, using all your gifts, talents, and life experience.

As author and teacher, Beth Moore says in her study on Esther, "There is treasure in your past that God wants to put square in the middle of your destiny. And contrary to what you might think or feel, God has chosen you for a specific purpose, not in spite of your history but because of it!"

As God took us through the Identity and Destiny: 7 Steps to a Purpose-Filled Life process, we had dramatically different experiences. Our most life-changing revelation through the process was discovering our God-given Identity.

I, Pam, discovered that I am a peacemaker. At first, I had a hard time believing it, yet looking back over my life, it became abundantly clear that this gifting had repeatedly played out in my life. I learned that when your greatest strength is unrecognized, it can quickly become your greatest weakness, going under-used and unappreciated.

Tom learned that he is a source of strength and focus and knew it was indeed the very core of his identity. Tom's challenge was to learn to moderate that strength and not overwhelm others with his intensity. He realized that his greatest strength must always be guarded and used wisely.

Once we knew our identity and destiny, God then gave us the assignment of writing and publishing *Finding Your God-Given Sweet Spot*. We understand it now, but when God gave us this assignment, it didn't make sense at all.

At that moment, as life and business coaches, we tell our clients the same thing we told ourselves, "You may not get it right now, but keep moving forward. Keep seeking God every step of the way and do the next right thing." As you do, your faith and trust muscles will grow strong, and you will build up your reliance on Him. God may ask you to do things you never dreamed of or felt worthy of being called to do. We persevered the publishing of our workbook and watched God perform miracle after miracle with our obedience.

Over the past 10 years, God has performed miracles with the Identity and Destiny program. We have had the privilege of building a worldwide network of thousands of followers and 150 trained coaches. Then God called us to pass the baton to the Nehemiah Project to steward Identity and Destiny, Finding Your God-Given Sweet Spot, into a whole new level. God called us to birth the program and then let it go. God had big plans for growth, and that is happening now in the hands of The Nehemiah Project.

Now it's your turn. It is time for you to find out who God created you to be. It is time for you to find out what He created you to do. It's time for you to find out your next assignment. It's time for you to discover your Identity and Destiny in Him. It will be life-changing. Remember, it's not about you, but the discovery process is up to you! Know you are worthy in the Father's eyes—do what you have been chosen and called to do! In Jesus' name, Amen.

For more information on buying the Identity and Destiny workbook and online courses and coach training classes, please visit nehemiahproject.org/.

A Note from Jim Brangenberg

In early 2012, a friend told me to go through Identity and Destiny, and I resisted. In the spring of 2013, I started the eight-week workbook process. Sixteen weeks later, I finished. God had revealed Himself to me and clarified my Identity, my Destiny, and my next assignment. iWork4Him.

Please take time and invest in yourself and deepen your faith by going through this life-changing study. Whether you do it online, in a group, or on your own, you will never be the same, and God will be more real to you than ever before.

Tom and Pam Wolf
Founders of Identity and Destiny

nehemiahecommunity.com/identity-and-destiny/

iWork4Him Podcast

- http://bit.ly/3hPfp3Q

17

Note from Drew Crandall

Northeast Christians at Work, Salt Mine

I HAVE A SOFT SPOT in my heart for everyday working Christians because I've been in the workplace for a long time—since 1972! From decades of experience, I know how challenging the workplace can be, day in and day out, through all the "stuff." It's relatively easy to be a Christ-follower at church on the weekend. But exporting, or integrating, your faith into the workplace is a challenge! Enjoy! – Drew.

This Is My Story

I grew up in the Tri-State area (Connecticut, New York, and New Jersey). This region tends to be a fast-paced, intense, and secular culture. I grew up in church, but what I experienced was religion, not a relationship. As a teenager, I left the church, went off to secular college, and launched my secular career. As an energetic high-achiever, I was eager to climb the ladder of success. Then during a breakfast meeting on Saturday, June 8, 1985, at 29 years old, I had my

"Road to Damascus" or "Come to Jesus" moment. I heard the testimony of a Christian business owner and was "born again." My faith in Christ came alive, and ever since that day, I've known that the Lord has called me to be a "minister in the marketplace."

During the first three years of my new life in Christ, I worked as an executive with an advertising agency. I was active in local workplace ministries operated by the Full Gospel Businessmen's Fellowship and CRU. Then, in 1988, the Lord called me into Christian entrepreneurship. As a small business owner, I joined the Fellowship of Companies for Christ International (FCCI.org), a ministry focused on Christian business owners and leaders. This peer-to-peer ministry impacted me greatly. During the decade of the 1990s, I led the FCCI ministry locally and regionally (FCCI-NE.org).

Continuing to make a living through my business, in early 2000, I launched Northeast Christians At Work (ChristAtWork.org) to influence a broader spectrum of Christ-followers in the workplace than "just" business leaders. Today, by God's grace, we serve thousands of working Christians through our media relations efforts, website, emails, social media, events, and special materials.

How We Can Help You

We intentionally make many of our resources *free*. For example, we currently offer a variety of free materials, including:

- Inspirational workplace posters (5), in either 8.5x11 or 11x17 PDF or hard copy sizes, you can display in your workspace. These posters are daily reminders to be a godly employer or employee and ongoing testimonies to co-workers. Our posters have been framed and placed on the walls of executive suites, used as content for national sales meetings, hung on office walls, shop floors, break rooms, church bulletin boards, and even tractor-trailer truck cabs!

- Encouraging one-page handouts (about 120), in handy 8.5x11 PDF format that you can study for personal devotions or small group discussions. These handouts contain helpful tips, Scripture passages, and perspectives about specific workplace topics and issues. They are used by Christian schools, adult Sunday school classes, workplace Bible studies, and staff meetings!

- Thought-provoking PowerPoint presentations (about 30) in PDF format on various workplace-related topics, which you can view, share, and print. These are especially helpful for people who participate in our speaking engagements and seminars, so they can prayerfully digest and apply the content afterward!

- Participation in our annual "Joy at Work Week" between Palm Sunday and Resurrection Sunday. You may download free church bulletin, sticker, and poster artwork. If you really believe what you say you believe, "Your Glow Should Show Who You Know!" People need to be reminded of the joy of their salvation. A consistently grumpy Christian is a contradiction of terms!

- Nominations for our annual "Northeast Marketplace Ministry Awards" leading into Christmas Day. We take nominations in different categories. There are no entry fees. Over the decades, we have honored hundreds of people and organizations. The press coverage generated from these awards has opened up opportunities for recipients to share their testimonies with others!

We also have a Speakers' Bureau and offer one-hour, half-day, and all-day seminars that can help you, co-workers, your church, and community. Our flagship seminar is the "Vibrant Faith @ Work Seminar," consisting of three consecutive one-hour sessions: *Unpacking the Cultural Landscape @ Work, Walking Circumspectly @ Work,* and *Being Christ-like @ Work.* Speaking engagements and conferences vary in pricing and structure.

If you do nothing else, please subscribe to our free "Salt Mine" email devotions, usually published on Wednesday mornings. These brief devotions inject relevant, fresh Scripture-based perspectives into your workday. For example, here are some comments from subscribers:

Hi Drew, very well said. The Lord has blessed you mightily with wisdom that you can apply to real life. Thanks for all your efforts and passion for God's Kingdom.

Thank you for that thoughtful email this morning. It was extremely timely for me. It's what I needed.

I can think of a few people who have very frustrating jobs who may need me to forward this to them.

Thank you for these words of encouragement always. I struggle with the drudgery of work, disappointment, and frustration and need to hear God's Word on this subject. I thank God he is using you in my life.

We also offer three soft-cover books:

- *Owner Talk, Owner Walk*: an interactive workbook on how to build a godly business for Christian business owners and leaders.

- *The Salt Mine*: a compilation of *Salt Mine* email devotions.

- *An Encouraging Word*: a compilation of *An Encouraging Word* newspaper columns about everyday topics.

Drew Crandall
Founder and President of Keep
In Touch, a marketing and media
firm, Founder of Jacob's Well
Christian Coffeehouse and
Northeast Christians At Work.

www.ChristAtWork.org

iWork4Him Podcast

- http://bit.ly/3s1a5yV

18

Note from Rich Marshall

God@Work *on God.TV*

IMAGINE MY SURPRISE a few years ago when the Lord spoke clearly in my mind: "Tell Dennis not to sell his business, but rather to begin to see his business as ministry." It surprised Dennis also, as he was quite sure that I was going to encourage him to "go into ministry." Well, I did, in fact, tell him to "go into ministry, the ministry of business!" That day provided a paradigm shift in my mind, and I have been telling business folks since then: "Your business is your ministry!"

Dennis, and thousands of others, have heard that word in their own mind, and today, some 25 years later, there is a worldwide movement called "Marketplace Ministry." Shortly after that, when I wrote my first book, *God@Work*, there were only a handful of books on the topic of marketplace ministry. Today, they number in the 100s!

One man, who was particularly impacted by that first book, found life and understanding in his struggle to both be in business and follow the call of God to be in ministry.

He and I became friends, and about five years ago, when he became the President and CEO of God TV, Ward Simpson asked me to join him and to produce a weekly program called God@Work. With this worldwide venue, we can share the power of God impacting your business around the world. God TV airs in over 300 million homes around the world! And my small part in that came out of simple obedience to tell a man, "Your business is your ministry!"

You can see over 100 episodes of God@Work on www.God.TV/work

I was a local church pastor for over 35 years, and they were good years, with growing churches and folks being saved and equipped for ministry. However, as fulfilling as those years were, these marketplace ministry years have allowed me to touch so many more people and see much more headway in the Great Commission. In addition to speaking to thousands through Marketplace Ministry conferences, God has also opened to door for ethics-based training in businesses, where hundreds more heard the salvation message "at work!"

I am so thrilled that Jim and Martha Brangenberg have identified thousands of men and women who work for Him and have interviewed them on their popular and powerful podcast. As I have reached retirement age (76), it gives me joy to look back see the value of God@Work. By the way, I am not retiring, I simply have reached the age where I could, but there is more to be done! Let's see the Great Commission fulfilled in this generation.

Rich Marshall
Author of *God@Work, Volumes 1 and 2; God@Rest*

www.GodIsWorking.com
www.God.TV

iWork4Him Podcast

- https://bit.ly/39cVisi

19

Note from Ford Taylor

Transformational Leadership

FORD TAYLOR DEVELOPED Transformational Leadership (TL) based on many years of experience from his own personal successes and failures. After getting a business degree from Texas A&M University, Ford and his wife, Sandra, acquired a struggling screen-printing business in 1982. Despite near failure, they were able to turn it around into a profitable business. This small company grew from a few individual investors to a $300 million operation, of which Ford was the CEO. Along with this career advancement and success, Ford became arrogant and prideful, which led to moral failure. After experiencing love and forgiveness, he decided to use what he had learned to help others.

Ford left his role as CEO of the company. He saw the need for leadership and stepped into the world of consulting and city reaching. Cofounding the ministry of Transformation Cincinnati/Northern Kentucky to unify leaders across the region to impact and improve local communities, Ford began to fully develop the TL model to teach leadership to bring success to businesses and organizations. As he continued to develop this model and work with companies, he realized that the reason it worked was because of the Kingdom/biblical foundations inside the material. This led to an additional training called The Missing Link (ML), which connects biblical principles to the original TL material.

Due to rising market demands, Ford founded the FSH Group. The organization is comprised of teams that provide leadership training and strategic consulting, with a vision to develop transformational leaders within every organization. They grow high-performing teams through teaching, training, equipping, and empowering high performing individuals with healthy relationships. Ford also leads an international charitable effort that provides TL to emerging countries worldwide.

The differentiated TL and ML trainings allow for teaching based on need. The team gives the biblical principles without connecting to Scripture (TL), or an organization can choose to include where the principles are found within the Bible (ML). Marketplace believers are shown how to put the Bible in a language that others can see and hear, which opens the door for the rest of the story.

Ford and his group have not given up on our world and fully believe in their vision that when leaders are given practical, implementable tools to teach, train, and equip, leaders will make leaders who will make leaders who will make leaders that can impact individuals, organization, cities, and nations. This will come as Christian leaders learn to humble themselves before God and submit to one another to see an accelerated convergence of synchronized destiny. In this place, we can influence the culture around us. When we see this and realize that we do not compete with one another but complete the Body by working together, look out, world, here we come!

TL can help lay a foundation for leadership with a few simple steps:

- *Vision:* Establish a clear vision
- *Serve:* Show leaders how they can serve their organizations to reach the vision
- *Teach:* Give new knowledge
- *Train:* Train with relevant experience
- *Equip:* Equip with the right tools
- *Empower:* Empower every individual within the organization to grow overall capacity
- *Let go:* Techniques to let go and allow each individual to fulfill their role
- *Evaluate:* Effectively give feedback on how the individuals are doing in their roles to achieve the vision

I am thankful for Jim and Martha Brangenberg and their relentless love and obedience in bringing an application to believers in the marketplace. It is so encouraging to be invited to work alongside them and "iWork4Him" as they continue to inspire unity with others to help their audience with so many tools and insights. What a blessing!

Ways to Get TL

Live Trainings: During the standard interactive two- to three-day leadership courses, FSH Group trainers equip attendees with practical tools and techniques to become influential leaders at home, work, and in their community. The goal of the training is for attendees to walk away from the live events ready to become the kind of leader they've always aspired to be. Individuals and teams achieve transformation by addressing and removing personal and professional constraints (TransformLead.com).

Consulting: Our consultants bring their personal and professional experiences to train the teams within your organizations and help you reach your specific goals. Our approach is to come alongside you and your organization to remove constraints and build high-performing teams (TransformLead.com).

Coaching: We provide personalized coaching. Are you the leader you want to be? Do people want to follow me? Am I a positive influence? We work with you one on one to get you to be the transformational leader we know you can be (TransformLead.com).

TL On Demand: Transformational Leadership and The Missing Link can be reached through a virtual interactive training platform called TL ON DEMAND. The online platform allows you to go at your own pace, or to participate with a facilitated group, to dive into the content (TLonDemand.com).

Book: Ford wrote the book *Relactional Leadership: When Relationships Collide with Transactions (Practical Tools for Every Leader).* This book gives the tools, techniques, and behaviors needed to become that kind of influential leader—

a relational leader—one who can lead toward profitability and productivity while cultivating a culture that attracts the best talent (FordTaylorTalks.com).

Ford Taylor Talks Podcast and Articles: During each episode of *Ford Taylor Talks*, you will be pointed to tools, ingredients, and behaviors that can be implemented right away to help with real-life issues and communication and to solve the constraints keeping you from being the person you want to be. If you want to *Love* the right way, have *Influence* with those around you, and *Transform* both your life and impact the lives of others (or as Ford Taylor says, "Get LIT"), this is the podcast for you (FordTaylorTalks.com).

Marketplace Solutions (Non-Profit): We want to advance the movement of (TL) Transformational Leadership by providing resources for individuals, organizations, and countries that might be prevented from experiencing these life-changing leadership tools. Whether domestic or in an emerging country around the world—we provide scholarships for our under-resourced participants and organizations. We have partnered with Marketplace Solutions to receive donations to help make this possible. We never want finances to be the reason anyone wouldn't be able to attend a training (4marketplacesolutions.org).

Ford Taylor
Founder of FSH Strategy
Consultants/Transform Lead
and Founder, Author of
Transformational Leadership and
Relactional Leadership

www.TransformLead.com
www.TLonDemand.com
www.FordTaylorTalks.com

iWork4Him Podcast

- https://bit.ly/2Lu6kBg

20

Note from Tracy Mathews

The Call to Work Course

FOR SOME, OUR JOBS can be taxing, stressful, and/or unful-filling. God has so much to offer us in our daily, hour-by-hour work situations—purpose, wisdom, peace, joy, and power—yet many of us don't know how to integrate our faith into what we do every day. Many church-based efforts are spent on equipping people to live as followers of Jesus in the church and with their families; however, they fail to prepare people in a similar way to follow Jesus in their workplace. Time spent at work typically consumes the larg-est share of waking hours and is one of our greatest arenas of character formation and external influence. God is pre-sent, and at work in every situation we face. Whether you work for pay or without pay, in the home, office, factory, store, school, hospital, bank, community, or any other sphere of society, God gives us our work primarily as a way to draw us closer to Him. Our work is a way to become more of who He has designed us to be and fulfill the pur-pose for which He created us.

About the Course

The Call to Work course is a workshop-based experience that teaches participants to attune to God's presence and guidance in their hour-by-hour work and life situations. The course teaches people how to put their faith into practice. It helps them respond to their daily situations and challenges, including the ones that keep them up at night—such as a difficult decision, a challenging co-worker, an ethical dilemma, and juggling work with other priorities—in better, more Christlike ways.

The course offers frameworks tools and a safe space for people to practice putting Scriptural wisdom into action, improving their response to specific situations. The ability to tune into God is a powerful skill, but it takes intentional practice. Through weekly practice and a prayerful pause, the course facilitates a habit and eventually character transformation toward Christlikeness. This growth fosters the fruit of the Spirit, brings greater fullness of life, and promotes enhanced mental, emotional, and relational capabilities.

At the heart of every course cohort is a Community of Grace. This safe space is marked by love, presence, acceptance, empathy, vulnerability, and a surrender to the Holy Spirit. We foster a posture of listening, where participants focus on gaining perspective but not judging or fixing. In a Community of Grace, we encourage one another to rest in God's love, forgiveness, and sufficiency. We let Him do the heavy lifting while simultaneously stepping out on faith, courage, and love as we allow God to lead us as we respond to life in new, more Christlike ways. With this practice, we grow in our ability and responsibility to help ourselves, and our patch of creation operates more according to God's will.

The Call to Work course is for people looking to:

- Grow and deepen their experiential relationship with God

- Jumpstart their spiritual growth and transformation

- Live a more integrated life where they can put their faith into practice every day and build the Kingdom of God through their daily work—promoting flourishing and the many facets of God's love in their workplace and community

- Grow in their ability to discern God's will, purpose, wisdom, peace, and power for their daily work and challenges, and follow it

Stories of Transformation

Story 1

I love my church and am passionate about God's calling to serve our impoverished neighbors. When the opportunity arose, I was thrilled to discuss a full-time position with our church leadership to lead and grow our church's local outreach and compassion initiatives. When I received the offer letter, the initial salary was much lower than expected, and I immediately struggled with feeling second-rate. Was this what church leadership thought of me and what I brought to the table?

I went through the Key Relationships Lens, and God met me there. He first helped me see that my salary does not equal my worth. He asked me to trust him. He then helped me see there is a fight to be fought—but it wasn't for my worth or salary. Instead, it was about helping our church grow in its ability to see the needs of the under-resourced populations in our community and learning together how to best walk alongside people with love and compassion.

In this, we not only serve those in need, but we grow in Christlikeness. God used the lens to lovingly show me that I had been way too self-focused and needed, instead, to think with the mind of Christ, trusting God with the outcome. At the conclusion of the lens, I felt a strong sense of God's affirmation of me and a green light to have a follow-up conversation with leadership born out of humility, authenticity, open-handedness, and love. God knows what our family needs, and I could trust He's at work in our church, leadership, and personal finances.

Story 2

Before engaging TC2W, I noticed a broken pattern emerge in my leadership and spiritual formation ... TC2W offered the framework, context, and activities for parsing this brokenness (i.e., what is good and what is broken in my thinking, feeling, believing, and acting?) and then discerning a more faithful way forward. It culminated with me writing a prayer to start my day and a simple prayer for when I sensed the broken pattern emerging.

Story 3

When I was searching for an example at work to practice the tools, my relationship with my dad kept cropping up. I realized it was something I had to address. We had been distrusting each other around the death of a relative and who should manage her estate. I wasn't trusting his intentions, and in turn, he wasn't trusting mine, and it was breaking my heart.

My dad's language was hurtful, and I wasn't sure if I could ever forgive him for treating me this way. As I walked through the exercises, recognizing how God is at work in this situation, it became clear that my dad's reaction was not about me but his own grief. The Christlike response was not to judge or be angry but simply let him know what it was like to be with this relative in her last days and reassure my dad that she cared for him.

Just after we completed the practice session and prayed for God's assistance, my phone rang, and it was my dad. I explained to him exactly what I had just articulated in the Kingdom Orientation Worksheet, with the assurance and honesty of a Christ-led heart, and my dad's response was beautiful. We shared a moment of love and appreciation, and I hung up the phone feeling like whatever I give up to God, no matter how hard it is when I apply these frameworks, the relationship outcomes will be fruit-bearing. I am so grateful for these resources. Thank you!

Tracy Mathews
Executive Director of
The Call to Work

www.TheCalltoWork.org

iWork4Him Podcast

- http://bit.ly/35kVXXt

21

Note from Kathy Book

Women in the Marketplace

WOMEN IN THE MARKETPLACE (WiM) is a ministry designed to help women integrate their faith in the workplace. Keeping our faith separate from our work-life limits our potential and, ultimately, the satisfaction we can find in our work. When we live an integrated life, we find purpose and lasting success. At WiM, we encourage small groups to meet weekly to build relationships and provide space to strengthen and encourage each other. Our curriculum is called *Unleashed*, a workbook that helps unleash the power of the Holy Spirit in your life.

The *Unleashed: Living a Fully Integrated Life* journey begins with our minds and the choice we have to invite the Holy Spirit into *all* of our work, not just during prayer or Bible study. When we allow our faith and relationship with God to be evident in all we do, we find incredible power and true purpose for our work. We understand the lasting impact we can have through our relationships and, ultimately, how to place our trust in God's plan for our lives.

Living a fully integrated life unleashes the fruit of the Spirit into every space we walk.

How did WiM begin? Through my personal story of discovering, I was *not* living an integrated life. I always thought I was a good Christian and a successful businesswoman. I was surprised when my manager pulled me into her office and said, "I know you go to church, serve at youth group, and feed the homeless, but why are you a different person when you are here at work?" As it turns out, I was a good Christian and a successful businesswoman, but not at the same time. I thought faith and work were two very separate entities.

God was certainly not wholly absent from my work. I would offer a prayer for co-workers in times of need, and I led a women's Bible study for some of my co-workers and friends over lunch. However, my manager's comment began to bring some questions to mind about my faith and work. Could it be possible that God wanted to be part of my *whole* life and not just the super-spiritual spaces I would set apart for Him? Was there a greater purpose for my work?

Over the next few years, I became aware that God wanted me to learn to trust Him and relinquish control of my life plan. As my trust grew, my faith did as well. This growth process ultimately led to the biggest risk and leap of faith in my life, letting go of a driven and successful 22-year career in Corporate America. I clearly heard the Lord tell me it was time to leave my job, be still, surrender control to Him, and trust He would show me what to do next. So I left an executive-level job without a plan, no new career path, and no one to support me financially.

Within days of the announcement that I was leaving, countless women approached me to set up a time to talk. They were struggling with the intense over-reaching demands in the workplace. They felt unsafe telling anyone, compromising time with family, friends, and self-care, all to try to succeed according to the world's standards. Some shared stories of wanting to quit but being too afraid.

My heart broke for the pain and isolation they were experiencing daily but hiding—just like I had. As I listened to these women I had worked alongside for years and realizing we were all struggling in silence and isolation, it began to feel like God had pulled me out so I could see more clearly how to help minister back into the place I just left.

Believing I was being led to help these women, I asked a few friends to get together to see if they would like to be part of a small group study. We ended up with three groups and decided to study Rick Warren's *A Purpose Driven Life*. Everyone liked it but still struggled with understanding how to integrate their faith in the workplace. I remember thinking, *I don't know either. That's one of the reasons I quit my job!*

I researched curriculum online and asked others, but no one seemed to have anything. I asked God for direction on what to do and heard Him say, "You write it."

I quickly responded, "I can't. I'm not a writer, I don't know the Bible well enough and certainly was never successful with living out my faith in the workplace."

Then He replied, "You can do all things through me."

I conceded and responded, "Yes. Ok. I understand, but you are going to have to show me how to do this."

Every single step was unknown and felt impossible. Not knowing how anything would turn out before taking a step forward left me fully dependent on God. Since I believed He was the one providing direction, moving forward in obedience was the only appropriate response. My confidence shifted from my ability to accomplish the task to God's ability to equip me. He gave me the following Scripture:

> … may He equip you with all you need for doing his will. May he produce in you, through the power of Jesus Christ, every good thing that is pleasing to him. All glory to him forever and ever! Amen. (Heb. 13:21 NLT)

Little did I know how foundational this Scripture would become in my life. Within a couple of weeks, He introduced me to three writers who would help make His vision for a ministry called Women in the Marketplace a reality. I met a blogger, a writing mentor, and a third writer who provided an outline for our curriculum. This would be the exact framework we needed to get started. Our current groups spent time brainstorming topics, and then I went away with an outline in hand to try and put together our first study. I had no idea what I was doing or how this would work, but God had a plan.

We have had the honor of witnessing countless stories of women growing in their faith and finding the confidence to trust God's plan in leading them to meaningful relationships and purpose in their current work or stepping out into something new. One breakthrough story was witnessed through our friend Mary.

On one occasion, Mary was struggling with a manager at work. She was frustrated and disheartened by the lack of support and the constant negativity she experienced daily. The toxicity of that environment was so profound that Mary wanted to quit her job. Her heart began to harden as she moved through the daily grind. She began to pursue opportunities outside the company and outside of the industry. Facing multiple roadblocks and rejections, she struggled with resentment, disappointment, and hopelessness. It started to consume her in every way, and she was ready to give up.

During one of her WiM groups, she felt prompted to share the story, unload this heavy burden, and simply ask for prayer. Very soon after that, Mary felt compelled to effect change. As she sat at her desk one day, she listened to her manager on a very sad phone call. Her initial thought was to walk away and disregard it. Instead, through the power of the Holy Spirit, Mary felt a tangible presence literally pulling her from her seat toward her boss. Words and grace flowed from her mouth that could only be recognized as the Holy Spirit speaking through her. She had the feeling that she was above the situation and watching while God was talking. What an overwhelming, awesome experience of God's presence. Even walking to the car later that day, she didn't feel like she had really returned from the experience yet.

Her heart toward her manager changed that day. Two lives were forever impacted by the power of the Holy Spirit, answering the prayer of a woman desperate for change. We don't realize it sometimes, but we are the ones God is trying to change. Having a small group where it is safe to share our struggles honestly, making room to pray for and with each other, allows space for the Holy Spirit to work. It allows our eyes to be opened to the hurting world around us so that we can offer our love and assistance. This is how we can begin living an integrated life and understand the real purpose of our work.

Kathy Book
Founder of Women in the Marketplace, Co-author of *Unleashed: Living a Fully Integrated Life*

www.WomeninMarketplace.net

iWork4Him Podcast

- http://bit.ly/38ojEQU

22

Note from Chuck Proudfit

At Work on Purpose

AT WORK ON PURPOSE began in 2003 as a small group of Christ-followers meeting together about work as worship. The number of participants grew steadily to become dozens, then hundreds, and eventually thousands of everyday working Christians from all over Greater Cincinnati, Ohio, USA.

At Work on Purpose has emerged as an innovative citywide workplace ministry model that mobilizes the Church at Work across church homes, denominations, zip codes, and ministries. While headquartered in Cincinnati, we are now supporting the development of citywide workplace ministry globally—in cities as varied as Dayton, Ohio; Minneapolis, Minnesota; and Nairobi, Kenya.

At Work on Purpose believes that every working Christian has an overarching purpose at work through the Great Commandment (Matt. 22:37-40) and the Great Commission (Matt. 28:19-20); that God has created good works in advance for us to do (Eph. 2:10); that we ultimately work for the Lord (Col. 3:23-24); and that God works alongside us as we pursue His purposes (Rom. 8:28). Our model for citywide workplace ministry has four distinctive and integrated characteristics:

1. *There is a holistic vision to restore the city's workplace for Christ.* In Greater Cincinnati, our headquarters city, the total population is about two million people. Of those, nearly one million are working or looking for work; and of those, about 350,000 are self-identified as working Christians. Only about 5% of working Christians consistently integrate faith and work, so right now, we have about 18,000 "faith active" working Christians. Our Big Holy Audacious Goal is that a day would come when all 350,000 of Cincinnati's working Christians embrace work as worship.

2. *Participation is ecumenical.* At Work on Purpose is intentional to build working Christian participation across church homes, denominations, zip codes, and ministries. We have a diversity of worship during the weekends, but we have the common cause of Christ through the workweek. While there is a natural tendency for Christians to segregate across traditional ministry lines, the workplace is an open space for spiritual connection and community.

3. *Ministry grows through a cultural network of influence.* Like the Early Church in the New Testament, workplace ministry has the flavor of an "Ekklesia" that sparks spiritual relationship and collaboration in a decentralized and organic way. The At Work on Purpose community is essentially a "network of networks" where working Christians can connect "needs" and "means" as they serve spiritually in the jobs, industries, and sectors where God has deployed them.

4. *Workplace resources are invested for the common good of the city.* Every Monday morning, the places where we go to work are spiritual mission fields. Our first focus is to "bring Christ to the cubicle," to be the Church at work. Beyond this, though, we have an opportunity to route some of the resources God grants us at work for the flourishing of the surrounding communities where we work and where we live.

The website for At Work on Purpose, www.AtWorkonPurpose.org, is filled with resource material, including the Mission2Monday study series on integrating faith at work; the Citywide Workplace Ministry in a Box toolkit; and the BIZNISTRY book on transforming lives through enterprise.

Chuck Proudfit
Founder and President,
At Work on Purpose

www.AtWorkonPurpose.org

iWork4Him Podcast

- http://bit.ly/3bjp1lW

23

Note from Darren Shearer

Theology of Business

THE THEOLOGY OF BUSINESS INSTITUTE (TBI), founded in 2015, is dedicated to the exploration and application of God's will for business.

TBI produces teaching and tools to equip marketplace Christians to disciple their co-workers, companies, industries, and communities through setting Christ-centered, Bible-based standards in business. As part of the broader Marketplace Christianity Movement, their vision is to participate in equipping every marketplace Christian with a Christ-centered, Bible-based framework for the work they do in the business world.

TBI's founder, Darren Shearer, realized the need for teaching the biblical-theological foundations for business after noticing a lack of teaching about business theology in most Christian business schools and theology schools.

TBI's podcast, the *Theology of Business Podcast*, and blog are the primary platforms through which its content is delivered. The podcast averages 1,300+ downloads per episode, and the blog receives 25,000 page views per year. Guests on the show primarily consist of Christian business executives and thought leaders in the relatively new academic field of business theology (www.TheologyofBusiness.com/podcast).

TBI's flagship course, the Biblical Standards for Businesses course (www.TheologyofBusiness.com/course), has been completed by hundreds of students from around the world. The course has been licensed to several colleges, universities, marketplace ministries, and peer advisory groups. In this course, students learn the following:

- How to articulate, explain, and apply the biblical foundations for the major disciplines of business: profitability and profit management, innovation, competition, value-making, marketing, sales, customer care, management, quality control, human resources management, accounting and accountability, business law, and risk management

- Why leading your company and industry in accordance with biblical standards is part of the marketplace Christian's calling to "make disciples of all nations"

- The current state of the "Marketplace Christianity Movement" and how to engage other Christians in this movement

Here are a few testimonials from students who have completed the Biblical Standards for Businesses course:

Thank you so much for the wonderful teaching! As I am so hungry for the material, I dove into all the teaching and finished it all in a few days. I will go back to study again and again. (Elaine Zhou, Singapore)

I was looking for a course that would teach how to apply the Bible to each aspect of business ... and this course was exactly that. (Walt Taylor, Atlanta, Georgia, USA)

This course was life-changing for me. I had a plan for my business ... but midway through the course, everything changed. (Sue Cavanagh, Alberta, Canada)

I thoroughly enjoyed the course, gaining new insight into operating a business. I think every Kingdom Entrepreneur should take this course. (Patricia Simes, Gary, Indiana, USA)

To help marketplace Christians identify their unique ministry roles in the business world, TBI has developed the Spiritual Gifts in the Marketplace Assessment. The assessment has been completed over 500 times and is presented to local churches as an alternative to the traditional spiritual gifts assessment aimed primarily at identifying volunteer opportunities on Sunday morning rather than mobilizing Christians for ministry in their workplaces throughout the week.

To help equip business leaders to run their companies, TBI has developed the Christ-Centered Company

Assessment as a tool to help Christian business leaders/owners align their company's business practices with biblical principles. TBI administers the assessment to companies on a consulting basis.

Rosedale College in Ohio is using the Christ-Centered Company Assessment as a tool to help their local business community as well as to provide mentorship to their current students. Local Christian business owners take the assessment with their executive teams; the Rosedale College students then interview those business owners/CEOs to learn best practices on how to run a business according to Christian principles.

Darren and TBI have produced two books for marketplace Christians: *The Marketplace Christian: A Practical Guide to Using Your Spiritual Gifts in Business* and *Marketing Like Jesus: 25 Strategies to Change the World*. Both books have been translated into Chinese and are being distributed among marketplace Christians in China.

Through their partnership with High Bridge Books & Media, TBI has also facilitated book publishing for the following marketplace-oriented books:

- *Christianity in Business: Applying Biblical Values in the Marketplace* (a product of Houston Baptist University's Center for Christianity in Business, Edited by Dr. Ernest P. Liang)

- *Bigger Than Business: Real-World Stories of Business Leaders Living Their Purpose* (by Jeff Holler)

- *Clarify: 12 Principles to Illuminate Your Calling to the Marketplace* (by Deneen Troupe-Buitrago)

- *Our Unfair Advantage: Unleashing the Power of the Holy Spirit in Your Business* (by Dr. Jim Harris)

- *Relactional Leadership: When Relationships Collide with Transactions* (by Ford Taylor)

- *The Christian Leader's Worldview: A Framework for Successful Leadership and Living* (by Michael LaPierre)

- *The Goldmine: Claiming the Workplace for Christ* (by Michael LaPierre)

- *Ambition: Leading with Gratitude* (by Seth Buechley)

- *Trading Up: Moving From Success to Significance on Wall Street* (by Jeff Thomas)

- *Marketing Like Jesus: 25 Strategies to Change the World* (By Darren Shearer)

- *The Marketplace Christian: A Practical Guide to Using Your Spiritual Gifts in Business.* (By Darren Shearer)

Darren Shearer
Founder and Director of the Theology of Business Institute, Founder and CEO of High Bridge Media

www.TheologyofBusiness.com

iWork4Him Podcast

- https://bit.ly/3pZPVDO

24

Note from Don Mencke

Real Christian Businessman

IT ALL STARTED WITH a challenge ... In late 2010, I felt the need to start using my past and present experiences to encourage others trying to balance their faith with their work.

I had just completed 18+ years in the secular music industry, trying to balance these exact two things. As I started my next job assignment working in the Christian publishing industry, my experience of balancing faith with my work came back to mind in a new and completely different way. I kept feeling I should start writing a blog.

I was not confident I would be any good at writing, or my experience and encouragement would make a difference. My superstar wife, always very encouraging, challenged me to go forward and start. She felt like other people needed to hear my encouragement and would be helped if I were writing a blog, sharing with others. But I was scared. No one would read my blog posts, would they?

The challenge came up again, when my good friend Jody and his family were visiting in March 2011. Jody also challenged me to get started writing a blog because he felt other people needed to hear what I was saying as well. He threatened to buy the domain name first if I didn't register it and start writing the blog within a week!

His challenge pushed me over the edge! I bought the domain name before he did, and it got me to where I am today.

I started out very timidly, though. After writing my first two posts, I only sent them to my wife and to Jody ... I wanted to make sure they sounded okay and made sense! They both encouraged me again to "send it to the masses," so I added almost everyone in my contact list to my email list.

Well, after nine years of weekly posting, I still have some of the original "voluntary" subscribers as well as a bunch of new ones too! Who am I? I am Don Mencke. I'm a believer in Jesus Christ (obviously!), a husband, a dad to two wonderful teenagers, I *love* basketball and all things tech, and can make a pretty mean homemade pizza.

Through my experience in both secular and Christian workplaces, God has given me a unique perspective to discuss balancing faith with my work. I design my blog posts so that "even I would read them." I keep them very short—between 350 and 400 words. They are also very practical—something the everyday businessperson or the CEO of a company can relate to when it comes to faith in the workplace. I give encouragement and advice to the believers in the workplace based upon my past experiences and what I am seeing in the world as we live it today. I would love for you to join me! Go to my website at www.RealChristianBusinessman.com and click on the subscribe tab, join my email list, and start receiving weekly encouragement. I also wrote a related 30-day devotional book called *Real Christian Businessman: 30 Day Field Manual Vol. 1.*

Don Mencke
Founder of Real Christian Businessman

www.RealChristianBusinessman.com

iWork4Him Podcast

- https://bit.ly/2LenHX5

25

Note from Ryan Haley

A Better Way

A BETTER WAY IS a ministry in the form of a business that helps people experience "where the supernatural meets the practical, by integrating faith with business and work." Our divine mandate is to manifest the goodness of God in measurable ways, emphasizing God's grace and rest. By focusing more on God's limitless abilities and wisdom than our limited human abilities and wisdom, we can all personally experience "A *Better* Way": God's design for *greater* success, but with *less* stress and *more* rest—and demonstrate that to other people. We create content and offer services that are equal parts spiritual and practical to help individuals and organizations live out their God-given calling and purpose. These include a book, podcast, coaching, financial services, speaking, blog, training, and teachings, all of which are designed to help people understand God's heart for them, as well as the purpose and joy God has for their work.

A Better Way is also practically oriented to equip people and organizations in the areas of personal finance, time management, investing, retirement, personal development, and business. The goal is to personally demonstrate and help others in "living a life that *demands* a supernatural explanation."[1]

God's grace is a combination of mercy (not getting the bad things we deserve), unmerited favor (getting good things we don't deserve), and divine empowerment (to live a life that would otherwise be *impossible* without God). With this amazing grace as the foundation of all we do and teach, bottom-line, measurable results always manifest as the effortless by-product of a revelation of God's grace.

Using the Word of God and the supernatural guidance of the Holy Spirit, A Better Way endeavors to help a variety of individuals, businesses, ministries, and other organizations discover greater peace, joy, and freedom. We help them get free of legalism and the self-focused demands of human effort to discover their own answer to this question: *What makes me come alive?* We help you find that answer by leading you to discover what we call your "Sweet Spot": the intersection of your deepest passion, deepest pain, greatest strength/gifting, and greatest service to others. The Sweet Spot is the life-giving place of divine purpose, resulting in deepest fulfillment and optimal effectiveness. As a result, the Sweet Spot is also the place of the most rewarding compensation: financially, professionally, personally, spiritually, relationally, emotionally, and intellectually.

A Better Way's purpose is to equip people and organizations to experience this first and foremost in their own lives, businesses, and work, serving as and leveraging their personal experiences as a powerful testimony of what is also possible for others through God's grace. We believe the best witness and apologetics for the gospel are lives and businesses that are undeniably blessed by God, inspiring and drawing unbelievers into a relationship with Jesus (and believers into a deeper relationship with Him). Our vision is for both the Church and the world to see God differently than religion has portrayed Him, through teaching and practically demonstrating the "[almost] too good to be true news"[2] of the gospel through the finished work of Jesus.

My Story

What has led me so passionately into this God-given calling is that I've spent most of my own life on the treadmill of self-effort and performance. My life changed dramatically when I crashed a US Navy helicopter, which ended my flying career and brought me to a low point in life. But it brought me into a renewed relationship with God and transformative life change. Perhaps the greatest change for me happened when I got a profound revelation of God's grace and the true essence of the gospel. This has given me much greater freedom and fulfillment in discovering and living out my own Sweet Spot and God-given passions in the pursuit of my divine calling and purpose.

A revelation of God's grace has transformed the way I think and has been applied to every area of my life, including business and work. As an entrepreneur who is very pragmatic, detail-oriented, and results-focused, I've been amazed at how God's grace and supernatural power also manifest in very bottom-line ways in business and life. I founded A Better Way to share this incredibly good news with as many people as possible, particularly as it applies to business, work, and finances. I've been encouraged and affirmed since then to meet many people whose lives and businesses have similarly been transformed.

Over the past few years, I've noticed that the Lord has given many Christians huge dreams and visions. Unfortunately, many don't know how to take the practical steps needed to partner with God and other people to step into their calling and live out those dreams God has planted in their hearts. I have seen through teaching, church, and classes that a deeper level of personal discipleship is necessary. My desire is to walk people through that process to become not only deeply fulfilled but optimally effective in their life's work.

To learn more about this revelation of God's grace and how it has shaped the story and personal testimonies of myself and others, you can check out my book (with a foreword by NFL Coach Tony Dungy, which is a testimony in and of itself!) called *A Better Way: God's Design for Less Stress, More, Rest, and Greater Success*.

Personal Testimonies

All-Cash Real Estate Investment with 44% Net Return in 2.5 Years

Despite conventional real estate investment wisdom advocating the exponential wealth-building benefits of using debt, God challenged me to believe for His best (which in this case was not to have to use debt of any kind). God opened doors I never would have thought to knock on. Through a divine appointment with a savvy real estate investor and consultant, I was able to find a "turnkey" property in another area of the country I never would've thought to look in. Using all cash, I was able to buy a four-unit multifamily property for $125,000 with a monthly rental income totaling $2,750. After owning the property for only 28 months, I was able to sell it *for a total net return of 44%!* By believing for God's best instead of following earthly wisdom, I am now not only debt-free but able to live entirely on passive income, partly as a result of this property. As 1 Corinthians 1:25 says, "… the foolishness of God is wiser than human wisdom" (NIV)!

Two-Week Vacation Leads to $825,000 Real Estate Listing Selling in Six Days

"He makes me lie down in green pastures" (Ps. 23:2a NIV). By submitting to the guidance of the Holy Spirit and *forcing* myself to take a two-week vacation (that I was worried would hurt my ability to generate business as a realtor and cause me to miss opportunities), God was working, while I was resting, to give me an amazing blessing.

The client was a family I was living with, and the wife strongly encouraged me to take the vacation. When I got back home, she said that I "looked different." For no apparent reason, she committed right then and there that whenever they sold their house, I would be their realtor despite their previous plan to use the 30-year veteran agent who helped them buy that house.

Several months later, this was my first listing, which sold for $825,000 within six days of being listed — to the perfect family we'd all been praying for. This resulted in the biggest check I've ever received! It all came by submitting to the conviction of the Holy Spirit and taking a "real rest" with Jesus (Mt. 11:28 MSG), prospering greatly from embracing the principle of "restful increase."[3]

Ryan Haley, MBA
Licensed Minister, US Navy Veteran, Founder of A Better Way as well as bestselling author, speaker, coach, podcast host, blogger, business school adjunct professor, and wealth advisor

ABetterWayPodcast.com
UnbridledWealth.com

iWork4Him Podcast

- https://bit.ly/3njW4st

---

[1] Reportedly said by John Maxwell (research did not definitively confirm this).

[2] graceLOVE blog article: "The Gospel – Too Good to Be True News" (http://gracelove.se/en/the-gospel-too-good-to-be-true-news/).

[3] Popularized by Pastor Joseph Prince.

26

Note from Bob Willbanks

Ambassadors for Business

I SPENT MOST OF my adult life "miserably saved," focusing on the "American Dream," success, riches, things ... with my get out of jail free card tucked conveniently in my back pocket.

There were many bright spots where I found myself at the top of the heap. There were even several occasions where I found myself worth millions, only to watch it all wash away due to my inadequacies and an insatiable desire for more. Throw an alcohol problem on top of my misguided life purpose and you can imagine the messes I would make for myself and my family.

The first real crossroads came in 1997 when I was divorced from my first wife, sold my shares in the payroll services business I had cofounded, and suffered three knee injuries to the same knee. It all culminated the night of the third injury with me lying flat on my back on my driveway, cursing God and telling Him I didn't want Him in my life anymore. I'd had enough. Obviously, it was all His fault, putting me through these trials. It was time for me to strike out on my own without God.

So there I was, relationally broken, professionally unemployed, physically encumbered, and spiritually barren. It wasn't pretty. I entered a period of darkness, which I have no idea how I ever emerged from alive and intact. I had split custody of my three sons, 11, 13, and 15 years old. They would be with me for four days, then over to my ex-wife for four. We only lived about a half-mile apart. On the surface, this was working out, but when I didn't have the kids, I was a mess.

On those days, I was usually drunk or high, starting at the local bar and ending up wherever "the crowd" would take me. I had money, generally buying rounds and striking up a party wherever I went. To those I surrounded myself with, I had it all. Nice house, fast car, money—I put on quite a show, all the while sinking deeper into the abyss of depression and alcoholism.

I had met Barb several years earlier via traveling baseball. Our sons had played on the same team. The new season in '98 started, and once again, our boys were playing together. As the season progressed, we built a friendship that began to feel special. I would find myself watching for her car, hoping she would be attending the game, allowing us time to talk. Late in the season, I finally asked her out, and the rest is history.

My relationship with Barb made me want to be a better man. I started to re-engage with my faith and take on a more responsible lifestyle. Then God sent church plant pastors who moved in right next to our home. We found an easy friendship with our new neighbors and began attending their church. I found a great mentor in Jan, the lead pastor, a man who thought deeply about Scripture and was a seminary professor in West Virginia.

He encouraged me to read the entire Bible in a year. I remember telling him I'd do it, then not following through. Year after year, this went on until he finally confronted me, saying, "I know why you're not doing it—it's because you can't." Well, that's all I needed. In 2003, I set my sights on reading the Bible cover to cover. I had to prove him wrong.

As I read, I was amazed at the content. I'd heard all the big stories about Adam and Eve, Noah, Moses, and all the others, but gaining the context by reading the entire Bible changed my perspective forever—all because a man got to know me well enough to challenge me in a way he knew would spark my desire. Thank you, Jan Linn!

I enjoyed reading the Word so much that I did it again the next year and the next, ultimately making over a dozen trips through the Bible using many different reading plans. Slowly, my life was gaining purpose, but I still had a problem, alcoholism.

During these years, Barb suffered through the roller coaster ride that comes with loving an addict. There were meteoric rises to the top of business and career, only to see it all slip away due to my drinking. I'd always seem to find a way to make a mess of things. Finally, in 2012 the Holy Spirit convicted me.

I'd had a bad month, the pressures surrounding the business were taking a toll, and I was drinking again, heavily. I remember I had three bad episodes over four weeks. When I say bad, I mean waking up in the morning wondering how I got home, who I had to apologize to, what happened? The third in the series had occurred on a Friday night. Saturday was a day of recovery. Usually, Barb would make these days miserable for me, but she mostly left me alone. On Sunday, I was reading the Bible (part of my daily morning routine), and I remember thinking, *Wow, Barb didn't get on my case yesterday. I wonder if I finally have her broken-in so I can do this anytime I want?*

That was when the Holy Spirit interceded, rising within me and saying, *"No!* God will never be able to use you the way He wants to use you with alcohol in your life!" I broke. With tears streaming down my face, I looked up to heaven and asked God, "Please, take this from me. I can't do this anymore."

He did. From that moment forward, I have never taken a drink. I praise God for the healing and am forever changed.

Miraculously, Barb came down to my office within seconds of this transformation. She sat down at my desk and asked:

"How are you doing?"

"I'm done."

"Done with what?"

"Drinking."

"Hah! For how long?"

"I'm just done."

"Okay, I'll give you another chance, but I'm not going to trust you for a long time."

I thanked her, we hugged, and life went on, but it was a new life. I took my faith seriously for the first time as an adult. I committed to Christian Business Men's Connection (CBMC) and joined one of their peer advisory groups. Finally, instead of running to the bar when things got tough, I sought answers from guys who were also serious about their faith. Iron truly does sharpen iron. I was growing at a fantastic rate, and God was prompting me to go deeper.

As part of this growth, I engaged in a study of Operation Timothy with Alan Smith, Northland Director for CBMC. I remember camping on the first question for months, "What is the purpose of life?" As I wrestled and sought answers for this question, my life's purpose began to gain clarity, finally culminating in my writing down my Life Purpose Statement:

> To use my God-given gifts, talents, and life experiences to impact the lives of others, so they may see what is possible in and through Him.

At the time, I was VP of Sales and Marketing for a large regional payroll company, which was soon acquired by a national company. After two years of struggling to embrace the new national organization, I decided to leave, starting up a consulting business that worked with business leaders to help them build margin into their lives. I would meet with leaders and connect them with other leaders as the Spirit led me. Occasionally, there would be something I could do for them, and it was enough to keep the bills paid, lights on. My faith was guiding my actions. Life was good.

In 2016, Alan Smith and Don Hoffert, leaders within CBMC Northland, encouraged me to start a Christian organization that would connect other Christians so they could do business together. After a few months of putting together a business plan, I launched Ambassadors for Business (AFB).

While putting the plan together, I was intrigued by Barna's research that found over 70% of America still identify as Christian. Why then were we experiencing a "post-Christian era"? Digging deeper into the research, I found the answer when I read that less than 7% of people who identified as Christian lived their lives based on biblical principles. Wow. This research finding sounds a lot like my past life, the definition of *lukewarm Christians.*

The initial mission of AFB was to focus on the lukewarm of our world, providing a place where they would be encouraged to reach for that next rung on their spiritual growth ladder while doing business with other Christians. Our mission was, "To equip Christians to walk boldly in faith as we connect them to do business together more efficiently and effectively."

AFB grew quickly, but like most non-profits, there was a lot of month left at the end of the money. Month after month, I began to sink into a deeper and deeper financial hole. Toward the end of April 2017, it got to the point where I had to lay it all down. I spent a full day unplugged, on my knees, in the Word, and on long walks. That night, while nodding off to sleep, I felt God's presence, like a warm blanket and a whisper, "I got this." I slept better than I had in months and can say that this experience gave me insight into what it means to have "peace beyond all understanding."

I generally wake up quickly, my eyes flutter, then my feet hit the floor, and I'm off and running for the day. In that split-second, I heard God's voice as I awoke the next morning. "Bob, it's not to equip, it's *equipping*, and that's an acronym for Engage, Question, Understand, Identity, Principles, Purpose, Integrate, Network and Grow." That was it—nothing more. I stood, momentarily incapacitated, thinking, "God?" Then my mind exploded—*that's nine letters, and it makes sense!* I ran to my office to write it down, and that's when I received the Ambassador Commitment that's etched on my heart:

> As Ambassadors for Business, we're meant to meet people where they're at, helping them EN-GAGE in a more intimate relationship with Je-sus Christ—encouraging them to ask life's big QUESTIONS so that they gain the UNDER-STANDING that their IDENTITY is in Him. Then, they can build their PRINCIPLES on the solid rock of the Bible, find their true PURPOSE in life, and begin to INTEGRATE with society as the salt and light God intended them to be. Building out their NETWORK for the Kingdom while GROWING in all aspects of their life.

Immediately following this revelation, AFB removed all membership fees and went completely donation based. Membership only requires acceptance of our Statement of Faith and Ambassador Commitment. Benefits include a fully enhanced listing in our online business directory, a RightNow Media@Work subscription, and access to nu-merous resources, events, and discounts.

These changes increased new memberships and facili-tated the launch of our Thrive! Connecting Faith and Work events around the Twin Cities, growing to 12 locations meeting monthly in less than a year. We've also launched our new G7 Networking groups, with the capability to train up leaders to lead Thrive! and G7 Networking anywhere in the United States.

I genuinely believe that AFB will be a global ministry, and we've been building the systems and infrastructure to make sure we're able to scale smoothly. It's this vision that continues to drive me forward. The opportunity we have to help people embrace their faith is an honor. AFB is the soil—yes, lowly dirt. Our job is to tend the soil—creating the fertile ground that allows people, businesses, churches, and ministries to thrive!

Let me add a final aside on my personal story. It was early in April 2017 when Barb and I were out running our Saturday errands together. I got back in the car after filling it with gas when she said, "Can I tell you something?"

A little unsure of the outcome, I stated, "Sure?"

She went on to tell me about her day. She'd been listening to a program about what you would be willing to do to keep another person in your life. She said it really got her thinking. Then she looked at me and said, "Bob, I would die to keep you in my life … I don't know if you know this, but five years ago, when you told me you were quitting drinking, I was coming downstairs to tell you I was leaving you. I was so serious about it I'd been stashing money away into a separate account. I know how hard it's been to get this ministry off the ground, and I want to put that money back into our account because, Bob, I trust you."

That's the power of the yoke of Jesus Christ. To me, the yoke represents the intimate relationship Christ wants from us. Focus on building that relationship, live a life centered on Him, and watch as He fills your life from the inside out.

Bob Willbanks
Founder and President,
Ambassadors for Business

www.AmbassadorsforBusiness.com

iWork4Him Podcast

- http://bit.ly/3ov3k6w

27

Note from Jeff Dorman

Breakthrough
*A Devotional Companion to
GiANT's Invincible System*

JOSH LANDED HIS FIRST major leadership position at age 34. He lived in the heartland of America and worked in a small division of a large corporation. Although well-educated, Josh realized he had much more to learn. This opportunity made him hungry to be successful and to help his team succeed. Josh knew that he and his team were good enough, but he wanted a breakthrough that would make them exemplary.

Josh heard through a friend how the practical tools and proven principles of GiANT Worldwide can make teams highly effective. The new Invincible system appeared just the ticket for him. Using the online video resources and worksheets with his team, Josh came to really understand his own "voice" tendencies and those of his teammates. This took their communication, understanding, and decision-making to a whole new level. As the year unfolded, the team worked through the 50 Sherpa training sessions while raising their productivity over 20%. Thanks to Invincible, Josh became a company hero. Even more important, Josh developed into a healthier man, a quality leader, and a better husband and father.

Unknown to his colleagues, Josh had an additional source of power to draw on in the form of his *Breakthrough!* devotional companion for the Invincible system. The Scripture, devotional, and prayer that integrated with each session helped unleash the power of his faith. The synergy of personal faith and insightful principles fueled his personal and professional growth. This empowered the breakthrough he had been seeking!

Faith multiplies the effectiveness of sound principles.

Individuals and teams are improving all over the USA and in over 116 other countries as businesses and organizations are discovering the benefits of creating *Invincible* teams through GiANT (www.GiANT.TV/success). And for Christians, the *Breakthrough!* devotional companion multiplies the effectiveness.

As a pastor for over 20 years, I know the power of unleashing faith alongside quality growth principles. Women and men like Josh working in the secular world can use this book in the privacy of their homes and boost their training through the integrated Scripture, devotional, and prayer for each session.

This book connects the inner life of our Christian faith and one of the best human development opportunities available. *Invincible* "unlocks the potential of people" and *Breakthrough!* unites those effective principles with the power of God, resulting in an absolutely transformational experience.

When does 4+4=16? When you turn the plus into a multiplication sign. When you multiply the Invincible principles by Faith, amazing things (dare I say miraculous?) can happen in an individual, a team, or an organization.

If only I learned this 20 years ago!

In nearly a decade of teaching GiANT principles and tools, time and again, I heard these words: "What an exceptional experience! I wish I had learned this 20 years ago. Then I (and those around me) would have been so much better off." Hearing people express regret for what might have been fuels my passion for lifting the next generation on our shoulders. I'm devoting the rest of my career to helping them be the healthiest, happiest, and most productive generation the world has seen.

Here is what people are saying about GiANT:

> Throughout the week, I have spent time with the 16 personalized videos for my "voice combination," and I have had a breakthrough in understanding myself. Clearly, the Holy Spirit is working in me through this program.

> The 5 Gears concept is equally valuable in the life of an at-home parent as well as the life of the CEO of a Fortune 500 company. Everyone can benefit from these tools.

I learned GiANT tools at work, but I am overjoyed with how they have helped my marriage. My spouse is delighted with my new communication and relationship skills.

The *5 Voices* system has transformed my supervisor. The atmosphere on our team has substantially improved!

The results from the *Invincible* system have been tremendous! Our people are developing great interpersonal skills, collaboration skills, the capacity to lead themselves well, and a greater ability to understand others.

GiANT taught us simple, scalable, and sustainable principles in a "sticky" visual-tool language that is accessible to everyone. It simply works!

Principles that were once expensive and available only to a few are now affordable and readily accessible for everyone since GiANT offers new a "Netflix-like" video-based platform. In fact, *GiANT's new Ascend program has hundreds of short videos that can be accessed for free!* (www.GiANT.TV/success).

The Breakthrough devotional wraps the GiANT training in Scripture, devotions, and prayers.

As a GiANT provider who served as pastor for over 20 years, I have spoken with many Christians who appreciate the value of the GiANT principles. But since the subject matter wasn't specifically tailored for religious settings, countless Christians were missing out on the blessings — until now!

Each week, one devotional sets your learning invitation before the Invincible video session, and a follow-up devotional challenges an investment in integrating the concepts into your Christian walk — at home, at work, in the community. Weekly discussion questions allow for small groups to journey together — church groups, home fellowships, Christian business owners groups, Christian university faculties, seminary students, etc.

The GiANT tools can be taken directly into the workplace, where you are free to bless others by helping them raise their level of emotional intelligence and teamwork. Your Christian witness will be strengthened as these teachings improve your relationships, enhance communication, increase productivity, and create a healthier workplace atmosphere.

A One-of-a-Kind Christian Growth Opportunity

How did this come about? After serving as a pastor for over 20 years, I was running my own business when a close friend told me about his work with GiANT Worldwide. I invested nearly a quarter century teaching, training, and discipling people in the church — where members spent perhaps one to three hours per week. Meanwhile, my friend was discipling people (without the Bible verses) in their workplace — where they spent 40–50 hours per week. Through our conversation, I caught a vision for the powerful transformation that can happen when a whole workplace of people is committed to learning together and supporting each other all week long. When I saw how beneficial the GiANT approach is for personal development, I declared: "I want to get involved in that kind of marketplace ministry!"

After joining GiANT and training hundreds of people over several years, the Lord challenged me to combine my pastoral experience with GiANT's teaching. The *Breakthrough!* devotional creates a Christian growth opportunity built on GiANT principles with profound practical application for everyday life.

Especially in this challenging time, I am committed to making materials available that will create a breakthrough—helping people develop a more Christlike character and become an even greater blessing to everyone they meet.

What kind of breakthrough are you seeking?

- To communicate effectively with everyone you lead...

- To be present and productive when there is never enough time...

- To get unstuck and move up to the next level...

- To become someone worth following...

- To increase your influence...

- To build an unbeatable team...

- To establish a healthy organizational culture...

Whatever breakthrough you are seeking, the practical nature of the GiANT training will help you know yourself to lead yourself better to empower you to become the spouse, parent, friend, leader, manager or employee, and community member you really want to be.

I believe that this devotional, along with *Invincible,* will provide a breakthrough for you!

How can you get started?

Simply visit www.breakthroughdevotional.com. There you will find a link to purchase the devotional book, as well as instructions to navigate GiANT's video platform (www.GiANT.TV/success).

Jeff Dorman
Founder of Dorman Consulting,
Certified Provider of GiANT,
Author of *Breakthrough*
devotional

www.breakthroughdevotional.com

iWork4Him Podcast

- http://bit.ly/2JWuVOQ

28

Note from Joe Carroll

Biblical Leadership with Excellence

SINCE 1985, BLE HAS helped thousands of working Christians relationally integrate their faith into their work with excellence and respect

Ministry Overview

- *Mission:* Helping People Connect with God's Greater Purpose in Their Work

- *Vision:* Mobilizing a growing, cohesive group of people in the workplace to be equipped as effective ambassadors for Christ.

- *Strategy:*
    - Connecting: Teaching how to connect with God relationally in work

- o Consecrating: Showing ways to consecrate all our work to God regularly

- o Commissioning: Empowering others to humbly represent God by serving others

Ministry Need: Some studies have shown that only about 30% of people experience purpose in their work. And of those people who do experience purpose, many are not pursuing work for the glory of God. Unfortunately, most Christians see very little connection and relevance on how the gospel of Jesus Christ can be authentically lived out in the pressures and stresses of the workplace. Christ came to bring fulfillment to all of life, including work (John 10:10).

Ministry Impact: In essence, BLE helps people experience "vocational discipleship." BLE events, small groups, mentoring, and resources provide unique insights and practical ideas that will help people to know Christ and make Him known in their vocational context. Through the BLE ministry network, workplace believers learn how to approach real-life work-related issues and benefit from personal interactions with experienced role models.

Whether you're a CEO or an employee, BLE will help you experience work as a calling and not just a job.

The BLE small group studies have had a remarkable impact on my marriage, my relationship with my kids, and my relationships at work. (Insurance Company CEO)

Being in a BLE small group at my office has enhanced my spiritual growth in the workplace ... it has had a great impact on my business relationships. (Senior Commercial Property Manager)

BLE has been helping (our church) develop discipleship-minded Christians understand God's purpose for their work and to view their workplace as His mission field. (Church Pastor)

Ministry Resources: BLE books, studies, materials, events, and videos can be found on BLE's website at www.BLEonline.org.

Joe Carroll
Executive Director, Biblical Leadership for Excellence and Partner in a prominent commercial real estate firm

www.BLEonline.org

iWork4Him Podcast

- http://bit.ly/39fg7Ud

29

Note from Bob Lambert
and Jennifer Reyes

Faith Marketplace Radio Chicago:
Bringing the Kingdom into Business

FAITH MARKETPLACE EQUIPS people in business with resources to bring the Kingdom into business while gaining
inspiration from marketplace leaders featured on *Faith
Marketplace* radio show and podcast. We've also created a
Kingdom Business Community for you to:

- Be in fellowship with other Kingdom entrepreneurs, business owners, and creatives

- Share powerful resources to enhance and
  embrace Kingdom impact in business

- Uncover powerful ways to create impact and
  glorify God in your business and those you
  work with

- Our website features the Faith Marketplace Kingdom Business Community:

  o Q&A with *Faith Marketplace* radio show guest speakers

  o Personalized training and discussions to help grow and scale your biz The Kingdom Way

  o Monthly group calls on Kingdom Business topics

  o Authentic connections built beyond traditional networking

  o Discounts or comps to Faith Marketplace events and more

Through the work we're all called to, we can move people closer to Jesus or away from Him, right? Some of the people we're called to serve are seeking godly examples of leadership. They're looking to us to see what it looks like to be a marketplace Christian. They keep watch of how we handle challenges and admit mistakes, how we thrive, and serve others.

Faith Marketplace has been making an impact for many years on air and is on the verge of Bringing the Kingdom into Business in a bolder way than ever before ... stay tuned! What *impact* do *you* want your business to have in the marketplace?

How Faith Marketplace Radio Hosts Bob and Jennifer Share Their F.A.I.T.H. in Business

F. For God's Glory: *What do you give God praise for in your business?*

Bob: I give God glory for the incredible grace and provision He has delivered time and time again.

Jennifer: Everything! It's not about me … it's all for His glory and the Kingdom! He showed me from the beginning of launching my business years ago how to show up in business, not as the world says but instead the Kingdom's way of doing business. There are no coincidences to who He connects me with and the people I'm called to serve. I would never have thought I would be leading people to open up their hearts to the Lord in business. I actually cried so hard when I first realized the gifts He gave me because I didn't want them and said, "Who am I to do this!" He quickly revealed it's **not** about me! I give Him praise for showing me what is truly a priority in business … God first, then to truly serve from the heart, help others break free from strongholds, ask for help and prayer, and be open to fully receiving.

A. Action: *How do you incorporate your faith into the work you do?*

Bob: I pray before I meet with people, ask God for His guidance in the conversation. I often include a scripture in my presentations, and through communication, refer to blessings. I look to acts of kindness and service I can provide in my interactions.

Jennifer: I work with people of all different backgrounds and beliefs. I let them know I'm not here to convince, convert, or condemn ... **and** I'm not going to shy away from speaking in truth with love. I share my testimony when and how the Holy Spirit leads me to. This often prompts people to engage in more in-depth conversations. I ask them thought-provoking questions and give them a chance to explain their viewpoints, pains, doubts, etc. and I **listen**.

I. Inspire: *How do you inspire others daily in your work?*

Bob: Because I am a networker and coach, I often look for opportunities to encourage, inspire, and comfort clients and others, especially when I hear they are going through a difficult time.

Jennifer: I ask God daily, who do you want me to connect with today? To encourage? To pray for? To serve? I am definitely a connector and like to bring people together. I've learned how to be a good steward of my boundaries and time and stay on mission! Many of my clients ask me to share with them how to honor God, especially in a world of so many distractions that try to pull us away from our calling and making a Kingdom impact.

T. Testimony: What is the story God wrote for you?

Bob: Years ago, God called me to Faith Marketplace to break down the walls between Christians in the marketplace. To inspire, equip, and encourage Christian business leaders to walk their faith in their leadership and interaction with their employees, customers, and vendors.

Jennifer: When launching Sales from the Heart years after being born again, I didn't realize I'd be led to share my testimony over and over again among a predominantly secular audience. But I followed the Holy Spirit's lead, and this is when I realized this is how I'm called to do business. God is working through me, and I work for Him. I thank Jesus for creating this path, and I walk it with Him and let Him correct my steps.

H. Hope: *How would you like to provide hope for others who are facing challenges in their business and life? (tips and resources of your expertise)*

Bob: I encourage Christians in the marketplace to get involved in Christian peer groups and look for a mentor who can inspire, encourage, and hold them accountable. Read the Scripture, leadership and motivational books, and articles written from a Christian perspective.

Jennifer: What does The Word say first? Let's go there before anything else. When I'm coaching, it's Holy Spirit led, and I've learned that I'm not always called to reveal the breakthrough even though I know what could be helpful. But the business side of things flows very easily for me, and I share that with my clients. If they are open, they begin to experience powerful shifts in how to do business for Kingdom impact and how God indeed calls us to do business.

We'd love to hear how *your* F.A.I.T.H. is making an *impact* in business! Message Bob and Jennifer 224-404-1988. We are always looking for great guests who have a Kingdom business story to share.

Our Story: How Bob and Jennifer Were Led to Co-host Faith Marketplace Radio Show and Podcast

- Bob Lambert was encouraged to host Faith Marketplace many years ago. With no radio experience, he stepped into this calling to inspire, equip, and encourage Christians to incorporate their faith and work. However, Bob didn't realize he was keeping his business and the show divided until he met Jennifer Reyes.

- Bob and Jennifer were brought together through a business ministry. Bob was seeking a way to collaborate. After praying, Bob felt that he needed someone to add a new perspective to co-host the show.

- Jennifer felt God nudging her to help Bob, and their radio show partnership began. Since being born again, she has been boldly sharing testimonies on how God moves in life *and* business. Together, their business

ministry has become a weekly encouragement to others.

- Bob and Jennifer have individual coaching
  and training businesses in addition to collab-
  orating weekly on Faith Marketplace. They
  provide a unique voice for encouraging and
  equipping people in business to share stories
  on how they do business in a way that glorifies God and creates Kingdom impact.

Listening to Faith Marketplace:

- Apple Podcast—https://apple.co/2TbuUrG
- Google Play—https://bit.ly/3bJEqZH

**Bob Lambert and
Jennifer Reyes**
Co-hosts of Faith Marketplace.
Bob is the founder of Samurai
Business Group. Jennifer is the
founder of Sales from the Heart.

www.FaithMarketplace.com

iWork4Him Podcast

- http://bit.ly/2Lz4jUi

30

Note from Chuck Bryant

Pinnacle Forum

WE LIVE IN A TIME of tremendous cultural upheaval when a biblical worldview is becoming less and less common. Every aspect of contemporary culture has been drastically shifting away from our nation's founding Judeo-Christian values—arts/entertainment, business, education, family, government/military, media, and religion—the seven mountains of culture. In this time of social unraveling and injustice, God is calling bold and courageous leaders, men and women—young and old, to join Him in transforming and preserving our culture.

The purpose of Pinnacle Forum is to encourage these men and women to grow in Christ, discover and discern God's call on their lives, and empower them to execute on that call. Forums are the foundation of what we do in Pinnacle Forum. Leadership can be a lonely walk, and many leaders exemplify the "lonely Christian leader syndrome." Our small confidential peer group forums are the vehicle through which deep relationships happen and from which we discover and help others discover and execute their unique calling in Christ for cultural transformation.

History of Pinnacle Forum

Pinnacle Forum was inspired by Dr. Bill Bright, founder of Campus Crusade for Christ International, who challenged a handful of leaders in 1996 in Phoenix, Arizona, saying, "I believe the only way we can change our culture is to find a way to network our high influence leaders and inspire them to use their influence for God."

Three of these leaders later hiked up Pinnacle Peak in Scottsdale, Arizona, and prayed that God would raise up leaders who would respond to this challenge and steward their influence accordingly. Their prayers were answered, and they began convening small peer groups around the city that aimed to encourage one another spiritually, share Christ with their peers, and challenge each other to use their leadership position and resources in strategic ways for the glory of God.

In 2001, Pinnacle Forum began to replicate this model throughout the United States, providing inspiration and the networking mechanism for leaders across America to magnify Christ. During the formative years of the organization, the foundation was laid in finding strong Christian men in or near the second half of their life ... men in high positions and at the pinnacle of their influence.

In early 2016, the first video forum was started on Zoom, allowing partners to meet from anywhere in the country. After a sputtering start, this concept began to increase as more and more forums started slowly. Soon they were meeting every weekday morning at times that were convenient for partners to attend in every time zone. By the time that the COVID-19 virus hit in 2020, there were 30 forums meeting on Zoom, and many more were started since then as people realized what an effective way it was to meet.

Pinnacle Forum welcomed women's forums into the mix with the launch of the first women's forum in 2013. A slow and steady growth began, and due to the first-ever held position for Director of Women's Forum Development in 2020, women's forums are growing rapidly. Pinnacle Forum's Young Successful Leaders initiative was also launched in 2020 with the first YSL forum and first-ever held position for Director of New Forum Development and YSL Forums. Raising influential leaders in their mid-20s and 30s is crucial to Pinnacle Forum's mission and will encourage bridge-building across generations.

My Story

My personal story with Pinnacle Forum began in 2005. I met CEO Ralph Pahlman, who told us about Pinnacle Forum. I agreed to help my friend Curtis Grant, a retired history professor, start the first forum in Modesto. We started meeting that fall in the offices of Vinson Chase, a local real estate broker. That forum met continuously in that same location for over 13 years.

I had no idea the impact the forum would have on me or that it would be the start of what has become my life's passion.

That fall, I was trying to sell my business. This was a time in my life when I felt very lonely and isolated. I could not talk to anyone about what was going on. If you have ever sold a business, you know what I mean. There are very few, if any, people who you can talk to about what is transpiring. With no one to talk to, I found in that first forum a group of men who had shared similar experiences, could keep a confidence, and would lift me up in prayer through some of my most difficult days.

This forum helped me realize the passion God had built into me that I had been inadvertently practicing in my business for years. I loved to help others find and develop their Ephesians 2:10 work that God had created them to do and then, with the encouragement of their forum, begin to live out that calling.

The business sold in the spring of 2006, and the guys in the forum suggested that since I had nothing else to do, I should spend my time working to help more forums in Modesto. With the help of Lloyd Reeb from the Halftime Institute in Dallas, who came to Modesto and did a seminar on finding significance in your second half, our first forum became three forums. Then Lance Wallnau came to Modesto and helped us understand the different spheres of culture. We continued to expand our forums until we had eight forums meeting at least one every day of the week.

In December of 2011, I was asked to join the Pinnacle Forum National Board and became board chair in December of 2013. I have had the privilege in the last 10 years of working with and learning from two Pinnacle Forum CEO's, Steve Fedyski and Guy Rodgers, and am currently serving as CEO.

At every juncture, I have seen God at work in Pinnacle Forum and me. We watch more and more people find the Encouragement and Equipping that comes from being in a forum, and the Engagement that comes from finding the work that God has created for you to do along with the Execution of that passion to do what God created you to do in the Encouraging atmosphere of a forum.

Partner Stories

On our website (https://PinnacleForum.com/pinnacle-pulse/), we publish monthly stories of partners and what they are doing and how Pinnacle Forum has impacted their lives. Please look at the stories of Ben Merkle, Johnny Parker, and Debbie Wuthnow. These three reflect an excellent sampling of what is currently happening in our forums.

Our Unique Position

Unlike so many marketplace ministries, ours is not specific to any area of culture. We are not exclusive to business, government, media, or any other corner of the marketplace. Pinnacle Forum caters to leaders from every area of our culture. It is a place for people to meet from different spheres of culture. We meet for an hour each week to encourage each other, pray for each other, and learn from each other. If you are a Christian leader in your area, we would love to have you join us.

Charles (Chuck) L. Bryant
CEO of Pinnacle Forum, longtime
Board Member

www.PinnacleForum.com

iWork4Him Podcast

- http://bit.ly/35hVR2S

31

Additional Faith and Work Organizations

THERE IS ONE CENTRAL coordinator of the Faith and Work Movement, and that is the Holy Spirit. He is busy stirring in everyday workers' hearts, revealing the call to incorporate their faith at work. New organizations continue to emerge to meet the needs in their cities and online.

While a resource list could never be complete, you have met several key leaders in the previous chapters. Here you will find some additional ministries to research and explore.

Find more resources at www.iWork4Him.com.

Listen to the Awaken Podcast Network at www.iwork4him.com/awaken-podcast-network#/.

- 4word women: www.4wordwomen.org
- Biblical Leadership: www.BiblicalLeadership.com
- CBMC: www.CBMC.com
- Christian Business Network: www.ChristianBusinessNetwork.com

- Christian Network Teams: www.ChristianNetworkTeams.com

- Christian Working Women: www.ChristianWorkingWoman.org

- Corporate Chaplains: www.Chaplain.org

- Doing Good at Work: www.DoingGoodatWork.com

- Dynatos Global: www.unleashbreakthrough.com

- Eternal Leadership: www.EternalLeadership.com

- Faith Driven Athlete: www.FaithDrivenAthlete.org

- Faith Driven Entrepreneur: www.FaithDrivenEntrepreneur.org

- Halftime: www.Halftime.org

- Heaven in Business: www.HeaveninBusiness.com

- His Way at Work: www.HWAW.com

- Kingdom Advisors: www.KingdomAdvisors.com

- Kingdom at Work: www.KingdomAtWork.com

- Kingdom Driven Entrepreneur: www.KingdomDrivenEntrepreneur.com

- Kingdom Way Ministries: www.KingdomWayMinistries.net

- Life Lessons Over Lunch:
  www.LifeLessonsOverLunch.com

- Lifework Leadership:
  www.LifeworkLeadership.org

- Made to Flourish: www.MadetoFlourish.org

- Marketplace Chaplains:
  www.mchapusa.com

- National Christian Business Roundtable Discussion Groups:
  - www.TruthatWork.org
  - www.C12Group.com
  - www.ConveneNow.com

- Nehemiah Project:
  www.NehemiahProject.org

- Right Now Media at Work:
  www.RightNowMediaatWork.org

- The Barnabas Group:
  www.TheBarnabasGroup.com

- Unconventional Business:
  www.UnconventionalBusiness.org

Part III

FINDING THE RIGHT resources can be the key to taking the proper next steps on any journey. When I started to understand that my work mattered to God, I looked for resources. I found books to read and experts on the subject. Before I could put my feet in motion, I had to find a place to start.

These resources are a result of my search and helped to shape our lives; I pray that they will jumpstart your journey.

iWork4Him core values include collaboration, connection, and transformation. We believe that sharing resources is key to all three of those values. Enjoy exploring these resources for yourself as they help you activate your faith at work.

32

iWork4Him: Faith and Work Recommended Reading

THE NUMBER OF BOOKS on the market is overwhelming. Each book has a purpose, but where do you start? Jim and Martha Brangenberg love to read and learn and have decided to share our Goodreads book lists with you. We hope this list of resources will influence your library and strengthen your resolve to grow with a biblical perspective in all that you do.

Jim's list includes only the highly recommended books that help incorporate the iWork4Him mission into daily life, at home, and at work.

Martha's list includes a diverse assortment of titles she has read to prepare for radio interviews, run our businesses, and grow in daily life.

Pick up a book today and be encouraged!

Are you looking to add to your reading list? *When you purchase through Amazon using this link* (amzn.to/3jhfht5), *you also help support iWork4Him!*

Jim's Favorite Faith and Work Titles
Top 10 Recommended:

1. *Monday Morning Atheist*, Doug Spada

   Do you flip the faith switch off when you head off to work on Monday?

2. *Upside of Adversity*, Os Hillman

   Adversity is used by God to take us from who we are to who He can use more effectively.

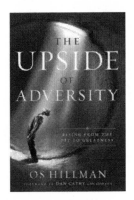

3. *Halftime*, Bob Buford

   Are you driving yourself nuts trying to pursue the elusiveness of Success? Try seeking significance in your success.

4. *God with You at Work*, Andy Mason

   The supernatural God at work in the marketplace.

5. *In His Steps*, Charles Sheldon

   People decide to ask "What Would Jesus Do" before making any business decisions. An 1896 classic.

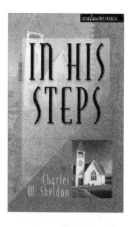

6. *Marketing Like Jesus*, Darren Shearer

   Jesus is the world's most outstanding marketer ever. His marketing plan is still in action, and it can help you form yours.

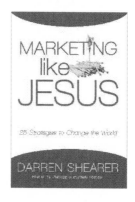

7. *Our Unfair Advantage*, Dr. Jim Harris

   The Holy Spirit was sent by Jesus to help us live our life in alignment with Him. Dr. Jim teaches us how to access that help in our work!

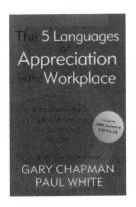

8. *The 5 Languages of Appreciation in the Workplace*, Dr. Paul White, Dr. Gary Chapman

   The world needs love, especially at work. When people feel loved, their whole work attitude is impacted.

9. *Today, God is First*, Os Hillman

   The very first devotional I read that taught me that my work mattered to God. Thank you, Os.

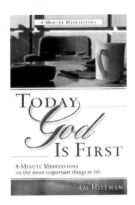

10. *Work Matters*, Tom Nelson

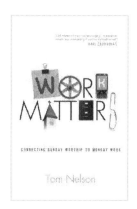

It is written by a church pastor for church pastors to encourage them to see their work on Sunday as equipping the flock for their mission field on Monday.

Martha's Favorite Faith and Work Titles
Top 10 Recommended:

1. *It's My Pleasure*, Dee Ann Turner

Chick-fil-A became successful because they treat their people right and their customers like special guests. Enjoy this inside look from their former marketing VP.

2. *Killing Wonder Woman*, TJ Tison

Working women of faith are subjected to daily blows of lies and deception. We are barraged with messages that we're not good enough, smart enough, thin enough, spiritual enough. We believe that our professions mean very little in the eyes of God. We're feeling tired and discouraged from holding ourselves to impossible standards. These damaging lies and labels now have a name: Wonder Woman.

3. *The 5 Languages of Appreciation in the Workplace*, Dr. Paul White, Dr. Gary Chapman

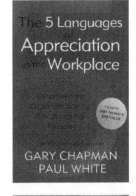

The world needs love, especially at work. When people feel loved, their whole work attitude is impacted.

4. *Proverbs for Business*, Steve Marr

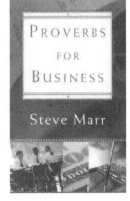

Daily devotionals that encourage and equip Christ-followers for living out their faith in their business.

5. *Faith in the Spotlight*, Megan Alexander

When you are on TV, you have a choice. Put your faith aside and the sky's the limit, or put your faith in the forefront and pray for a miracle. Megan got that miracle.

6. *Stretched Too Thin*, Jessica Turner

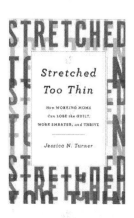

Christian working women have it tough. Christian working moms have it tougher. Where do they turn when things seem to be spiraling out of control?

7. *For Women Only in the Workplace*, Shaunti Feldhahn

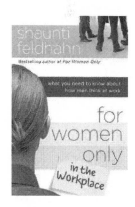

Even the most experienced Christian businesswoman can inadvertently sabotage her career simply because she doesn't know how her male managers, colleagues, and employees think. Shaunti provides startling insights into the expectations and perceptions of men at work.

8. *Master of One*, Jordan Raynor

What is your one thing? The entrepreneur thought leader and best-selling author of *Called to Create* offers a refreshing invitation: stop trying to do it all so you can thrive in your unique, God-given work.

9. *The Janitor*, Todd Hopkins, Ray Hilbert

When a retired executive gets bored with being at home, he gets a job as a janitor. He ends up discipling and mentoring the CEO after hours.

10. *The Switch*, Doug Spada

Introducing the 55 million Christ-followers to the idea that their faith and work should be intricately connected, Doug Spada focuses on shifting our thinking from TGIF to TGIM and promoting a No Moan Monday.

Visit www.iwork4him.com/book-list for more recommended titles.

33

---

16 out of 1,700 Stories
from the Show

Stories of Faith at Work

THE *IWORK4HIM* TALK SHOW began in the spring of 2013 and now has well over 1,700 episodes recorded. We've curated a list of 16 episodes to start you on your listening journey with *iWork4Him*. Meet some of our guests, hear their story, and then subscribe to iWork4Him on your favorite podcast platform.

Find all of the options at www.iWork4Him.com/podcast.

1. Luke Andrews

Over the years, we have watched Luke go from being a mortgage/real estate/insurance/investment advisor to going all in for Jesus in his businesses and living out iWork4Him. Now listen to Luke trying to change the world through Biblically Responsible Investing.

Show Description

Stop following the world's ways and let God transform you by renewing your mind and changing the way you think, even when it comes to retirement and investing. We're talking with Luke Andrews of Inspire Advisors about Biblically Responsible Investing (BRI) and why he became a financial advisor.

- www.iInvest4Him.com
- http://bit.ly/2L1OOEP

2. Chelsea Drinkard, CBWC

Chelsea saw a need. Christian working women are in desperate need of support as they live out their faith in their work. Christian Business Women's Connection is that ministry, and Chelsea is on fire for Jesus as she operates as a commercial real estate broker.

Show Description

We had a great hour with Chelsea Drinkard of Office Space Brokers on being single. Give today's podcast a listen and hear the inspiring story about how God uses her "singleness" every day for His glory.

- www.CBWCTampaBay.com
- http://bit.ly/38lr338

3. Bill Wolf

Bill takes over his dad's plumbing company and grows it into a mechanical empire. Bill's generosity and his love of his employees have transformed the air conditioning industry in Tampa Bay.

Show Description

Local business owner of Midway Services, Bill Wolf, is in the studio to talk about how his Christ-centered focus is at the heart of his business, how this focus shapes his work environment, and what it means to truly work for Him, which he has been doing since day one—and it hasn't always been easy.

- www.ThinkUtilityServices.com
- http://bit.ly/3niaj16

4. Kathy Branzell

From primary education teacher to the president of the National Day of Prayer Task Force, Kathy has led the way for spreading love all over the nation through relationships and prayer.

Show Description

Kathy Branzell is on a mission to bring the love of Jesus to every American, and she needs your help. Love2020 looked to touch every person in the US with the love of Christ by the end of 2020. Here how, and why, in what Jim calls an "earthquake in the marketplace" on today's massive program.

- www.Love2020.com
- http://bit.ly/38kdgKi

5. Skip Stanton

One day Skip's co-worker invited him to lunch. He shared Jesus with him, and Skip's life has never been the same. Skip now runs his company focused on the ministry part of every customer transaction.

Show Description

We dove deep today into the faith walk of Aqua Plumbing and Air's owner and heard how Skip's journey with Christ has "changed his paradigm." We also got a look at how he came to be within his profession, which makes him a great boss (with a special guest chiming in), and his work with C12. It was a powerful hour of discovery and witness.

- www.AquaPlumbingSarasota.com
- http://bit.ly/38nLOeP

6. Jamie Vrinios

Once in the top 10 of sales for a huge cosmetics company, Jamie has seen adversity. She was asked to leave her career because of her faith and personally dealt with breast cancer. Jamie's difficult life path all started in her childhood. Her story highlights how God has rescued her time and time again.

Show Description

We had the pleasure of having Jamie Vrinios share her faith story of going from utter poverty to the highest levels in a national MLM organization. Check out today's podcast to hear what the Lord is laying on her heart now as she faces her halftime and seeks Him to find "What's Next."

- www.JamieVrinios.com
- http://bit.ly/2JZu8g8

7. Todd Hopkins

Todd ran a commercial cleaning company and realized that his faith was the center of his enterprise. He decided to franchise and base the entire company on living out faith in Jesus in every aspect of the company. Twenty-six years and six books later, Todd has 135 franchises where thousands of employees are loved-on every day as they clean commercial properties.

Show Description

The first time on iWork4Him, Todd Hopkins talks about taking his faith public.

- www.OfficePrideFranchise.com
- http://bit.ly/3hR5gUd

Show Description

We were jam-packed on the radio today as Todd Hopkins with Office Pride Office Cleaning joined Jim to invite four young men who've been moved to action by the mission of CBMC Young Professionals. Check out today's show and hear how the Lord is moving in these young men's lives. These guy's faith is impacting their work in a **huge** way.

- http://bit.ly/2LwkaTT

8. Nancy McDonnell

Growing up in the rust belt, Nancy saw some pretty difficult times for the region's people. To bring healing to the steel and coal industries, Nancy decided to teach companies to value the people they hire.

Show Description

Nancy McDonnell, and friends with the ministry "The Value of the Person" out of Pennsylvania, joined us to talk about the awesome power of love and its impact on employees and organizations.

- www.ValueofthePerson.com
- http://bit.ly/398cYp7

9. Mark Pearson

Mark desires to think big and challenge norms. In the financial industry, he realized that most people need clarity on why they invest in certain companies. Nepsis Capital is a nationwide organization focused on Kingdom transformation and helping investors to invest with clarity.

Show Description

Long-time friend and owner of Nepsis Capital, Mark Pearson, joins Jim to talk about their personal and business relationship, how Mark works to keep Christ at the center of his investment decisions, and how that financial paradigm is imperative for financial success.

- www.InvestWithClarity.com
- http://bit.ly/3s3YoHJ

10. Kali Davis

Kali Davis never had a problem trying to live out her faith in her work in middle management. Working for companies big and small, Kali understands the ministry field God has placed her in.

Show Description

Live from Rogers, Arkansas, at this year's Workmatters Conference to highlight business leaders and their stories of how this conference—and the mission of Workmatters—has reshaped their work-life. This team leader from The Harvest Group shares her inspiration in this episode.

- www.Workmatters.org
- www.HarvestGroup.com
- http://bit.ly/38p9gIq

11. Tim Paskert

With a heart and passion for film making, Tim Paskert decided that his God was big enough to fund the filming of *The Glass Window*. This movie, now seen by millions of people, inspired Tim and his team to develop short YouTube films that challenge people to think about reality and faith in Jesus.

Show Description

From a life of atheism to making movies glorifying the Lord, Tim shares his incredible story of becoming a Christ-follower and what it's done to his vision and inspiration. You'll also hear about his latest work, plus a special guest opens the show with Jim to talk about his recent talk with the Christian Chamber of Commerce—Tampa Bay.

- www.Mark829.com
- http://bit.ly/3hR5ZEV

12. Rick and Holly Betenbough

I don't cry easily, but these two interviews moved me to tears because of the genuineness of the story of Rick and Holly Betenbough. Rick and Holly run a very successful home building company. When God hit Rick upside the head about his ministry to 170 employees, Betenbough Homes has never been the same.

Show Description

It's the "Kingdom Leadership Workshop" in Lubbock, TX, where we'll be broadcasting from *live* this week, and we kicked it off with return guests, Rick and Holly Betenbough, to get their take on this amazing workshop and hear how God's been moving them.

- www.KingdomAtWork.com
- http://bit.ly/39eRbMi

Show Description

We interviewed Rick and Holly Betenbough with Betenbough Homes (Tx), and boy howdy, did they share from their hearts. They're working for Him by showing His Love through *everything* they do, top to bottom. Hear about their beginnings to how they interact with their staff and customers (*amazingly*), and why they chose to follow Him in *all* they do in our program that shows the iWork4Him mission statement in action.

- http://bit.ly/3seBPAm

13. Paige Murrell, #2 Show of All Time

She left me speechless. It has only happened twice on the air, and Paige was the guest both times. Paige was 17 when we did this interview, and she taught an audience of iWork4Him

thousands to connect their faith and work intricately. Flourishing and worship, both words you don't hear about work often, but you will in this show.

Show Description

On a very special 500th edition of the program, Jim invites contest winner and young artist Paige Murrell, whose whiteboard story sketch on one's calling won an award at the Institute of Faith, Work, and Economics, to talk about her artistic passion, what drives her heart and mind, and her inspirational thoughts on the idea of a calling.

- www.TheStorySketcher.com
- http://bit.ly/3otBRlu

14. Queen, LSD, and Bikes, #1 Show of All Time

I thought this show might have ended our time on the air. You see the title. We opened the show with Queen's "I Want to Ride my Bicycle" and then show guest Jon Dengler shares how he met Jesus on an LSD trip. It gets even better from there.

Show Description

We took our bikes out today (figuratively speaking, of course!) as we invited the leaders of two great bicycle-centered ministries in the studio to detail how they're using wheels to talk about Jesus. Super cool! Patrick Simmons with Bikes for Christ, and Jon Dengler with Well Built Bikes

— 266 —

are hopping on the saddle and riding for Him! Grab your helmet and roll with us!!

- www.bikeshoptampa.com
- http://bit.ly/38o9jUN

15. Dr. Jim Harris

No single book title has revolutionized my thinking more than the book by Dr. Jim Harris, *Our Unfair Advantage: Unleashing the Power of the Holy Spirit in my Business*. Retired executive and highly sought-after speaker Jim Harris now uses his platform for challenging all Christ-followers to understand why the Holy Spirit is given to us by God.

Show Description

Do Christ-followers have an advantage over their non-Christ-following business counterparts? Dr. Jim Harris believes so and lays out why in his new book — *Our Unfair Advantage* — and talks on the show today about how, and why, the Holy Spirit should be a part of your everyday work life.

- www.unleashbreakthrough.com
- http://bit.ly/3nk5yE5

16. Ashton Batten

When you combine Jesus and chocolate, you get this favorite, as Martha loves M&M's. Ashton brings her fresh millennial perspective of living out her faith in a huge company and knowing that she is a workplace minister along the way.

Show Description

We used our time at this year's Workmatters Conference in Rogers, Arkansas, to grab a bevy of interviews to highlight how Jesus is moving within the hearts, minds, and work-spaces of all sorts of workplaces. Today, we heard how this exceptional millennial found faith in a very sweet place.

- www.Workmatters.com
- http://bit.ly/3ookxOF

34

The iWork4Him Trilogy

IWORK4HIM: CHANGE THE WAY You Think About Your Faith at Work is part of a trilogy that God has put together. The other two titles are *sheWorks4Him: Embrace Your Calling as a Christian Woman at Work* and *iRetire4Him: Unlock God's Purpose for Your Retirement* (which we co-authored with Ted Hains). These books are a collaborative effort with dozens of contributors specifically focused on giving practical, tactical, factual, and biblical perspectives to the Christian working woman, everyday believer, and the retiree. You will find each of these books has a unique perspective that will continue your journey or help someone you know grow where they are. Go to www.iWork4Him.com/bookstore to find all three books.

sheWorks4Him Introduction

I am so excited for you to read *sheWorks4Him: Embrace Your Calling as a Christian Woman at Work*. Each chapter has been written by a Christian working woman who has been our guest on *The iWork4Him show*. We have heard their hearts on the air and asked them to share their unique work experiences in this book. Each chapter also includes thought-provoking, spiritually challenging questions designed to help you shape your perspective as a Christian working woman. These can work in a small group of trusted friends or just with you and the Lord all alone.

Why did we do this project? Because as a Christian working woman, you need to know you are not the only one struggling to live out your purpose in your work. We learn a lot from other people's faith stories, so it is our hope and prayer that each chapter helps you feel more celebrated, validated, understood, and resourced for living out your faith in your work.

I have never met a woman who wasn't working hard, trying to be everything to everyone. Your workplace may be at home or in a high-rise; almost all women suffer from trying to do it all. TJ Tison describes this complex in her book, *Killing Wonder Women* (TJ wrote a chapter in *iWork4Him: Change the Way You Think About Your Faith at Work*). We want you to embrace who God created you to be, not fulfill the expectations of culture or the church.

God has given you a unique set of gifts, talents, and abilities. Your spiritual gifts are from Him. First Peter 4:10 NLT says, "God has given each of you a gift from his great variety of spiritual gifts. Use them well to serve one another." He gifted you to do the things you are doing. He placed you in the workplace you are in because He needed and wanted you there. You were called into the world to be a living and breathing example of the Gospel in your work. As you turn each page, you will see how God has led these Christian working women to serve in their job more effectively, using their unique giftedness.

Sisters, you are a gift and a blessing. With your busy schedule, it's easy to let your priorities suffer. Remember this. Your number one priority is growing in your life with Christ, getting closer to the Father every day. All other priorities seem to fall in order when we keep Him as our number one.

The amazing women who wrote each chapter are willingly sharing a part of their story to both encourage and challenge you. I pray that it will launch you with renewed purpose in your workplace mission field.

—**Jim Brangenberg**, Talk Show Host and Mentor, www.iWork4Him.com

iRetire4Him Introduction

There is a thread of mentoring stitched through the many phases of my life. In seventh grade, my youth pastor invested time in my life and introduced me to the narrow path paved by Jesus. In high school, a college student mentored me for several years. In my early 20s, two business couples invested their lives into Martha and me, guiding us on the unique path of being an entrepreneurial couple. In my 30s, several pastors devoted time from their busy schedules to help keep me on the narrow road. And in my 40s, God blessed me with several mentors to reveal the significance of my work as a ministry. Today, I have three men that love the Lord and invest their time to help me to serve God the best way possible.

Mentoring changed my life and can change the trajectory of any life. It is powerful, it is personal, and it is purposeful. Jesus used it with His 12 disciples and the 72. Investing your life in that of another is the way to most closely mirror how Jesus spent His time on earth.

I am not retired. I don't know if I will ever officially be retired by the American definition, but living in Florida has allowed me to meet a lot of retirees. Most of my friends, neighbors, and fellow church members are retired. These friends have shared some of their life perspectives with me. They feel like they are off the field and have been placed in the grandstands of life. They feel relegated to watch the youngsters run the plays of life while they sit back and miss all the action.

iRetire4Him: Unlock God's Purpose for Your Retirement is a call to those in the grandstands to come back on the playing field of life, to mentor those running the plays. The opportunity to mentor the next generation is abundant and brings the personal purpose reminiscent of a job well done while allowing the flow of unrestricted faith. *iRetire4Him: Unlock God's Purpose for Your Retirement* is dedicated to helping you find faith-centered purpose in your retirement as you live out the best days of your life. Powerful, personal purpose can be found by investing your life into the life of another, in the form of mentoring.

Ted Hains adds impactful stories to the end of each chapter, and you will also meet some great ministries that embrace retirees. Join us on an incredible journey of preparing to live with purpose, investing in others, and joyfully declaring iRetire4Him. I am asking you to spend your retirement years mentoring the next generations. You may be the parental figure referred to in this scripture.

> My son, obey your father's godly instruction
> and follow your mother's life-giving teaching.
> Fill your heart with their advice and let your life
> be shaped by what they've taught you. Their

wisdom will guide you wherever you go and keep you from bringing harm to yourself. Their instruction will whisper to you at every sunrise and direct you through a brand-new day. (Prov. 6:20–22 TPT)

—**Jim Brangenberg**, iWork4Him

35

Commit Your Life to Jesus: First Time or Recommitment

I BECAME A FOLLOWER of Jesus at 13, while my youth pastor was mentoring me. I made this decision after seeing that life on my own was headed towards a dead end. Jesus said in John 10:10, "The thief's purpose is to steal and kill and destroy. My purpose is to give them a rich and satisfying life" (NLT). I had seen the thief's work in my life. It left me empty and hopeless. Jesus's plan for my life was the answer I was looking for. I think you will see why.

—Jim

The following pages by the Pocket Testament League will help you understand God's ultimate rescue plan for you. This is what changed my life.

If you would like a copy of the Gospel of John, send an email to Jim@iWork4Him.com.

A True Story in Your Hands

The Bible is an eyewitness account of history that has stood the test of time and made a difference to billions of lives around the world.

- Have you ever wondered why you are here on earth?

- Have you ever had a sense that you were made for more?

- Have you ever been amazed by the beauty of this world? Or the wonder of love? While at the same time also being shocked and discouraged by the hatred and evil around us?

There's a Reason You Feel This Way ... You Were Designed for Good

God created the world, and that includes you—and He declared everything He made to be good! In fact, He says you're "very good" because you come from Him!

That longing you have inside yourself for the world to "be right" may seem like an echo—here one moment and gone the next—but don't be confused, that sense of longing comes from God.

Not only do you come from God, but you have purpose. The Bible says that your purpose is to be with God in a world of love and beauty and meaning.

We know that something is wrong—and it is us. It's me and you.

Without God, we choose to live for ourselves. You might think of it as walking away from God.

The Bible calls that *sin*. Take a moment and ask yourself, "Do I do things I know are wrong?"

If we are honest with ourselves, we will admit we rebel … we sin.

When we sin, we break our relationship with God. And everything that was meant for our good gets broken.

Can We Fix This Problem?

Great question! We cannot. Many have tried. Many try to build a bridge to God.

Have you ever tried? Tried to live perfectly? It's impossible, right?

The problem is BIGGER than you may realize. Sin separates us from God forever.

But God Intervened Because He Loves You!

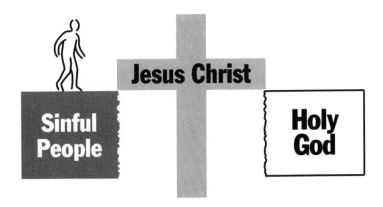

> For God so loved the world that He gave his one and only Son, that whoever believes in Him shall not perish but have eternal life. (John 3:16 NIV)

What you can't do through your own efforts, God the Son, Jesus, did by coming to earth to die on the cross for you. He took the punishment for your sin. Jesus became the way between God the Father and you. Jesus Christ is the only way for us to reach the Father (John 14:6).

What Does All That Mean?

- It means that you can have a real, meaning-ful life—today and forever. "I have come that they may have life, and have it to the full" (John 10:10 NIV).

- It means that when you believe in Jesus, you are restored to the "very good" relationship you were created for... you become God's son or daughter. "Yet to all who did receive him, to those who believed in his name, he gave the right to become children of God" (John 1:12 NIV).

- It means that you can live with passion and purpose because you walk in a loving rela-tionship with the One who created you, serv-ing Him and sharing the Good News of His love with others—reconciling the world to God.

How Can I Know God?

There are three steps to take:

1. Admit that you need God and turn away from sin (see John 8:11).
2. Believe (have faith) that when Jesus died on the cross, He took the punishment for all your sin, and He rose to life again to conquer death (see John 1:29).
3. Receive (ask) Jesus Christ as your Lord and Savior.

A Simple Prayer

Here is a prayer to receive Jesus Christ as your Lord and Savior. It is a suggested prayer. The exact wording doesn't matter, what counts is the attitude of your heart:

> Lord Jesus, thank You for showing me how much I need You. Thank You for dying on the cross for me. I believe that You are who You say You are and that You rose from the dead to conquer sin and death. Please forgive all my failures and sins. Make me clean and help me start fresh with You. I now receive You into my life as my Lord and Savior. Help me to love and serve You with all my heart. Amen.

Jesus said, "Whoever comes to me I will never drive away" (John 6:37 NIV).

What's Next? It Depends

If you prayed the prayer, congratulations. Becoming a follower of Jesus is only the beginning of an exciting adventure. You are invited to read this entire Gospel of John, turn to the back of this booklet, and sign that you've responded to Jesus's call. We've included some additional pages with what to do next and links about where to find resources for the journey ahead.

If you are not ready to respond to Jesus's call, consider reading about Jesus. When people would meet Jesus and ask him questions, his answer was, "Come and see."

So, come and see. You're invited to meet Jesus.

Read the Book of John. If you don't have a Bible, email me for a Book of John—jim@iWork4him.com

The Book of John is an eyewitness account of the life, death, and resurrection of Jesus of Nazareth. John wrote this account with a special theme in mind that he states near the end:

> But these are written that you may believe that Jesus is the Messiah, the Son of God, and that by believing you may have life in his name.
> (John 20:31 NIV)

My Response

If God has spoken to you and you are ready to follow Jesus, fill out this page as a reminder of your response.

I hear God calling me, and I now know that my sin separates me from Him. Because God loves me, He sent His Son, Jesus Christ, to pay the penalty for my sin by dying on the cross to restore me to fellowship with God. I have asked Jesus to forgive my sins and give me eternal life. It is my desire to love Him and obey His Word.

Name _____

Date of Response _____

Visit www.ptl.org/response and let us know about your life-changing response. We'll send you information about free resources you can use to grow closer to God.

Follow Me

Jesus loves people and people are curious about Jesus. Jesus's solution is simple. Follow me. For centuries, people have been doing just that—following Jesus.

Becoming a follower of Jesus is only the beginning of an exciting journey. Jesus called it being "born again" (see John 3:3). It means that you now have a personal relationship with God as your Heavenly Father. You are not alone. God sent the Holy Spirit from Heaven to be your Counselor, to guide you into all truth (see John 14:26; 15:26; and 16:12–15). He will help you live each day for God and to accept the changes He wants to make in your life. You can depend on His power to enable you to grow as a follower of Jesus.

Being a follower of Jesus involves a whole new life. Start now:

- √ *Read* a part of the Bible each day.

- √ *Pray* daily; talk to God as you would to a close friend.

- √ *Worship* God by attending a church where the Bible is taught.

- √ *Join* with other followers for support and encouragement.

- √ *Share* your faith in Christ by offering people one of these Gospels.

Want to learn more? For a free course on the Gospel of John or to join The Pocket Testament League as a member (membership is free), visit www.ptl.org/follow.

About the League

The Pocket Testament League is an interdenominational evangelical organization founded in 1893 when a teenage girl and her friends made a commitment to carry pocket-sized New Testaments to share with others. The League encourages followers of Jesus everywhere to Read, Carry, and Share God's Word. Learn more about The Pocket Testament League by visiting www.ptl.org/about.

Statement of Faith

The Pocket Testament League adheres to the following statement of faith:

- † The inspiration and authority of the whole Bible (Old and New Testaments) as the full revelation of God by the Holy Spirit.

- † The Deity of the Lord Jesus Christ, His virgin birth, His substitutionary atoning death on the cross, His bodily resurrection, and His personal return.

- † The necessity of the new birth for entering the Kingdom of God, as described in John 3.

- † The obligation upon all believers to be witnesses of the Lord Jesus Christ and to seek the salvation of others.

Reach the World for Christ! Join the Movement

If God has spoken to you through His Word, join us today. Go to www.ptl.org/join and click on JOIN NOW. If there is a number in the box below, enter it in the Referral ID field *when you sign up.*

Take the 21-day challenge. Read through the Gospel of John and grow closer to God. Track your progress with your personal dashboard and earn points as you Read, Carry and Share God's Word in the form of pocket-sized testaments. Visit www.ptl.org/marathon to get started!

THE POCKET TESTAMENT LEAGUE®
PO Box 800
Lititz, PA 17543
www.ptl.org

More from iWork4Him

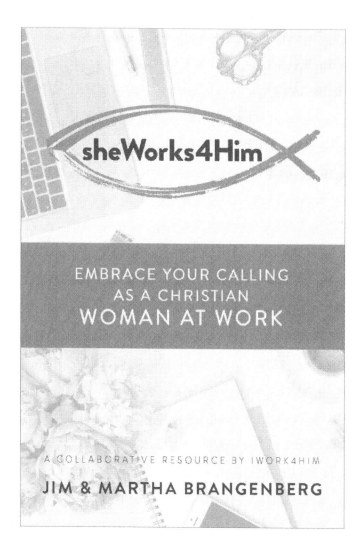

For the retiree in your life